Payments: Dancing in the Dark

... an insider's insights

Payments: Dancing in the Dark

... an insider's insights

If you aren't talking with people from stakeholder groups that can impact your success, then you're just dancing in the dark...

on the edge of a cliff!

Foreword

A note from the author

When I met my husband, I was surprised that he didn't have all the music he had recorded, but he said that by the time an album was released the band was back in the studio working on the next one - and didn't think about the last one. The same is true of the work that most of us do. We're focussed on our current assignments and have little time to think about the past.

I joined ACT Canada in 1990 and suddenly it was 2017. Over those years I became the defacto historian of the Canadian payments market. Many people suggested I write a book about it, but for one thing I was too busy and for another I couldn't imagine who would want to read it. That isn't to say there aren't rumours, scandals and a number of buried bodies (or at the very least, dead careers) but it isn't my place to share them.

Now that I have time I've put together a year by year look at the market and the association that brought about so much change with, and on behalf of, stakeholder members.

Why? By looking back I was usually able to predict the future, and now when payment is growing more complex, your career might benefit from the same hindsight.

My thanks

First and foremost to my husband Rick, who supported everything it took to survive and thrive. To Andrea McMullen, who shared the journey and carries the legacy forward.

To Rick Adamson, David Chaudhari and Paul Zatychec; three chairmen of the board who taught me so much and inspired me to be better - I will always be grateful for your guidance and friendship. You made the difference.

I am also appreciative to all who supported the work of the association and even to those who opposed us, because they can be credited with adding to the steel in our association backbone.

This book is dedicated to Rick Belanger and Andrea McMullen, who made this journey possible.

Catherine
2019, 01, 14

Contents

What's in this book for you?

To succeed - to stand out from the pack - you need strategies and insights. This book gives you both.

Payment has become complex in the past 25 years and promises to stay that way, but you can predict where it's going by looking at past trends. Add to that an understanding of your market and the best practices that separated winners from losers over those 25 years, and you are well on your way to success.

To understand any market you need to know not just what people are talking about, but also what questions they're asking and who they trust to give them the right answers. Who's talking together and where are they meeting? I've often gleaned insights from company sign-in books and conversations happening in out-of-the-way restaurants at conferences. As you go through each year in the market review you'll see what stakeholders were talking about, who they were talking with and what various governments asked us to comment on. This will give you a better understanding of how the market progressed and you'll notice patterns develop over the years. <u>Those patterns will help you predict the future</u>.

Dancing in the dark

Neglecting to talk with others who can impact your success is like dancing in the dark – in a mine field!

I had thousands of conversations with acquirers, issuers, law enforcement officers, merchants, payment networks, regulators, suppliers and consumers over the years. They helped me understand payment in a way that couldn't have been possible without access to every stakeholder group. As a result ACT Canada predicted what would and wouldn't work with uncommon accuracy. Using that same market knowledge I'll share my predictions with you on where payment is headed.

What this book delivers

The book starts with 10 best practices, strategic tips and insights. I've watched key market shapers use these consistently to advance their projects and their careers.

The early chapters then take you through a high level history of payment and give you a glimpse into the future. They look at how organizations leverage the knowledge and resources of others and how individuals do the same to advance their careers. The insights chapter features editorials that offer timeless advice and warnings.

I encourage you to read through the year by year review. Each year's key highlights and market notes give insight into how we saw the market and what market shapers were embracing or struggling with. From this you'll get an understanding of what did and didn't work and again, you'll see patterns.

Each has a list of headlines from the year's news as published by ACT Canada. These too show what the market was doing. It should be noted that it doesn't include the thousands of headlines from stories that revealed the accomplishments and breakthroughs by companies that supply and support the payments industry. Without their pioneering work we could not be where we are today.

The past is a roadmap to the future used by many successful people.
Welcome to the past, present and predictable future of payments.

For you – dear reader

On a personal note, it was only by putting this information together that I could understand the impact of the association on the market and our members. My heartfelt thanks to all who helped us "ACT on behalf of our members".

I wish you happiness, health and the focus and discipline that bring success. I wish you challenges that will help you grow. I wish you the satisfaction of taking ownership and responsibility for your work and your life. And I wish you the overwhelming joy of doing things for no other reason than they are the "right" things to do!

I wish for each and every one of you - time. You can always make more money but you simply cannot make time.

I wish you time to think ahead. Almost everything we do has future steps. When we think about them, plan for them and consider how to protect those steps from the risks they may face we have a future. When we don't think about how to make things better in the future we only have the present.

I wish you time to reflect on those things you do remarkably well. Often they will be things that come easily to you, but that does not take away from the accomplishment. Allow yourself to recognize your strengths and then work to improve your other skills.

I wish you time to reflect on your relationship with others; your friends, family and the people you may never meet, but could influence. Do your best for all of them through your personal life and professional work.

I do not need to wish for you success, because if you spend your time well your success will be immeasurable.

Best Practices, Strategic Tips and Insights

After analyzing hundreds of successes and failures of the past 27 years of payments, here are the top 10 I've picked to help you and your company thrive.

1. Identify other stakeholders who will be impacted by your work and talk with them because they can influence your success. There is also a high likelihood that they are working on plans that could impact you. The objective is to understand each other's goals, plans and processes. When you do that you can cut costs, get to market sooner and mitigate risks.

2. Be sceptical of pundits' market growth and size projections. History shows that most (if not all) have been wrong over the past 27 years. Unbridled enthusiasm can lead to investing too much, too soon.

3. Focus on what consumers will pay for, not what technology could do. The only other legitimate reasons to innovate are to force your competitors to make similar investment before they are ready, to avoid fraud, to be compliant with regulations or to prepare for a subsequent innovation that will result in revenue and profits. While the latter are reasonable reasons to innovate your shareholders will be happier with innovations that consumers will pay for.

4. Build security and privacy into your products / services and feature them in your marketing. Consumers are increasingly concerned with both security and privacy. If you build them but don't talk about them you run the risk that consumers will perceive your product or service is risky to use.

5. Always know what problem your innovation will solve. Too many innovations offer something different, not something better. If you can't identify or articulate the problem you'll have a hard time selling your "solution".

6. Focus on the consumer experience not the payment. No-one gets up in the morning and says, "Today I'm going to pay for things". Make the payment consistently easy!

7. Be careful. When you rush to be first to market make sure that you won't be the first to fail. Identify potential dead ends and ask lots of questions.

8. Remember, too much innovation in the marketplace can be counterproductive. Studies show that consumers may be interested enough in your product, but if there are several new things available they may not take the time or have the inclination to compare them – finding it easier to stay with the status quo.

9. Stakeholder engagement and management is a critical business issue, and never more so than in an emerging market. Successful people know that there will always be times when competitive interests will drive the agenda, but they are also wise enough to know that many of the things needed to develop a healthy market benefit from collaboration among stakeholders. They work together to build or protect a market in which they can then compete.

10. Payment is complex! That means that many innovations will fail and many careers will stall. On the other hand, you can be a break out star if you adopt the best practices.

What do I base these on? You'll know as you read this book. One last thing – I have an 11th tip and it applies to life, not just payment. You'll find it on page 38, in an editorial titled, "What I learned from Colonel Chris Hadfield." It is *everything you need to know to succeed* no matter what you do for a living or who you work for.

Payments: From Cave Man to the 20th Century

Payment has always been, and always will be, a part of daily life. This chapter shows that its development has been evolutionary and slow, responding to market needs. For today's payment professionals, it gives a hint as to how the evolution will play out in the coming decades.

In the beginning

It all began with
>...You have that
>I want it
>...I have this
>You want it
>...Let's trade!

Barter - or trade - was the earliest form of payment.

This cow is getting heavy

Barter had some drawbacks. You couldn't always find someone who had exactly what you wanted and who also wanted what you had, so there needed to be a way to buy or sell just one thing. Then there needed to be a way to pay for that thing. Metals such as gold and bronze, salt and other spices were all used. They were easy to carry and rare enough to have measurable value.

 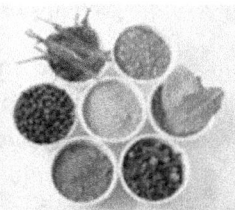

To coin: a phase

King Alyattes of Lydia (now Turkey) introduced the first official currency in 600 BC; a coin decorated with a roaring lion. Earlier parts of China introduced small bronze replicas of various goods in 1100 BC. Where metal working was not yet available, shells or ivory jewelry were often used because they were divisible, easy to store and carry, scarce and hard to counterfeit.

In 1250 AD, Florence minted a coin called the Florin that was widely accepted across Europe. At the time this facilitated commerce but it was long before agreements were reached on how payments would work.

The early regulators

As people and governments started to look at things that would represent value, laws had to be developed around their use.

Babylonians and their neighboring city states developed the earliest system of economics with rules on debt, legal contracts and law codes.

This was followed by:

- the Codex of Ur-Nammu (circa. 2050 BC)
- the Codex of Eshnunna (circa. 1930 BC)
- the Codex of Lipit-Ishtar of Isin (circa. 1870 BC) and
- the Code of Hammurabi (circa 1760 BC)

These law codes laid out the role of money establishing amounts of interest on debt, fines for failure to comply and compensation for various infractions.

These coins are getting heavy

In China paper money was first issued by the Tang Dynasty in 740 BC but it did not last. The Song Dynasty re-introduced it in 1024 AD. By the 12th century paper money was commonplace.

Unfortunately over printing led to inflation. Throughout the following centuries there were several episodes of inflation causing China to abandon paper money after hundreds of years of using it.

Banks also began issuing paper notes that circulated in the same way that government issued currencies circulate today. In England this continued up to 1694 with Scottish banks issuing notes until 1850 and the US through the 19th Century. At one point more than 5000 different types of bank notes were issued by various American commercial banks but only those issued by the largest and most creditworthy banks were widely accepted.

These banknotes could be converted into gold or silver at the issuing bank, opening the door for potential problems. Since banks issued notes with value in excess of the precious metals they kept on hand, unanticipated requests for conversion that surpassed that could result in a loss of public confidence in a bank. In turn, that could trigger a mass exchange of banknotes by customers and result in what came to be known as a "bankruptcy".

National governments gradually replaced private commercial banks as banknote issuers. The Bank of England was granted sole rights to issue them in England after 1694 and in the US the Federal Reserve Bank was given similar rights in 1913. These currencies were partially backed by gold or silver and were theoretically convertible. This is no longer the case.

On March 10, 1862, the first United States paper money was issued – before the Federal Reserve Bank became the sole issuer. The denominations were $5, $10, and $20. They became legal tender by the Act of March 17, 1862.

Canadian play money?

In the early days the government of France supplied metal coins to its colony in Canada but they were hard to find because people hoarded them, preferring to pay in animal hides. Early trappers used hides as money, but settlers hoarded the rare coins knowing that if they wanted to buy manufactured products from France they would need to pay with them. Ironically, coins sent to Canada by the government of France often left by the same boat on which they came.

To make matters worse, the annual boat from France that brought goods and metallic coins usually came in the summer but in 1685 it didn't arrive until the following January. Coins meant to pay the troops were 8 months late. This meant the Governor from France had to find an interim pay solution and he decided to issue fiat money, using playing cards.

After requisitioning all the playing cards in the colony he had each card cut in quarters, wrote a monetary value on each piece, signed and stamped them. He decreed that these had to be accepted in payment for everything that was for sale in the colony. When the boat finally arrived in January each and every card piece was exchanged at par against metallic coins and the card pieces were then destroyed.

It worked so well the first time that the Governor repeated the process every year, issuing more and more cards each time. Sometimes paper was used instead of playing cards because they had become hard to find. The quantity of cards or paper multiplied leading to 400% inflation in 1713.

Before the French, indigenous people had a well-developed barter system. Their wampum belts were used for various reasons and traditions - but not as a form of payment. Europeans however did use them as a kind of currency and colonists even started to manufacture their own.

Fast-forward more than 100 years. Canadian banks began to issue bank notes with the first from the Montreal Bank (now the Bank of Montreal) in 1817. Other banks, such as the Bank of Upper Canada, the Bank of New Brunswick, the Bank of Nova Scotia and the Bank of Prince Edward Island followed suit.

In 1841 Canada issued pounds (similar to the British currency) but they faded away in 1858 when the government decided to adopt the decimal system.

In 1866 the Province of Canada began issuing its own paper money, in denominations of $1, $2, $5, $10, $50, $100 and $500. $20 bills were introduced in 1934. The Dominion of Newfoundland issued notes from 1901 until it joined Canada in 1949. The basis of comparison for the early Newfoundland notes was the Spanish dollar and as a result they had a higher value than the Canadian dollar.

Canada was created in 1867 by the British North America Act, 1867 and originally had four provinces; Ontario, Quebec, New Brunswick and Nova Scotia. The federal Parliament was assigned exclusive jurisdiction over "Coins and Currency", as well as "Banking, Incorporation of Banks, and the Issue of Paper Money" with control over coins and notes centralised in Ottawa.

As the Bank of Canada became established, the federal government gradually reduced the power of chartered banks to issue their own notes. The last chartered bank issued note for use in Canada was a Royal Bank of Canada five-dollar note in 1943. Old banknotes were gradually withdrawn from circulation and in 1953 the last remaining power to issue banknotes (for use outside Canada) was abolished, with the Bank of Canada becoming the sole issuer.

A $1 coin, nicknamed the "loonie" and a $2 coin (the "toonie") replaced the comparable notes in 1987 and 1996 and pennies (1 cent) coins were taken out of circulation in 2012.

Author's note
There are many sources of information on the history of payment and not all agree on dates. The point of this chapter is to show that payment has evolved since the time of the cave man and will continue to do so. Most changes were to solve problems with the existing payment processes of the day.

Payments: The 20th Century and Early 21st

This chapter looks at key changes in the payments market from the early 1900s to 2018. As you look at products and services that emerged and went on to succeed or fail, you'll see patterns. They will help you evaluate new opportunities.

Why payment history matters

From bartering, in vogue for more than 12,000 years before the emergence of "hard cash" in 1100BC, through to today – there are certain trends that will most likely carry on as payment continues to evolve.

Customers want payment methods that are easy to use, accepted everywhere they want to shop, and secure. For a new payment product or service to succeed it must offer an improvement to one or more of these.

To their credit...

Fast-forward to America circa the 1800s. As Americans migrated west, some merchants used credit coins and charge plates to extend credit to local farmers and ranchers so that they could delay paying their bills until they harvested their crops or sold their cattle.

In the early 1900s a few stores made money by offering proprietary credit cards to ensure their customers' loyalty and maintain sales. Bank-issued charge cards began in 1946 when a Brooklyn banker named John Biggins launched the Charg-It card. The bank was the middleman, reimbursing the merchant and obtaining payment from the customer. Charg-It cards were only available to the bank's customers. New York's Franklin National Bank followed suit, issuing its first charge card to loan customers.

Diners Club needed a different way to make money since, unlike stores, they weren't actually selling anything. To make a profit without charging interest (interest bearing credit cards came much later), companies that accepted the Diners Club card were charged 7% for each transaction and card holders were charged a $3 annual fee as of 1951.

The company focused on signing up salesmen as customers. Because salesmen often needed to dine (consequently the new company's name) at numerous restaurants to entertain clients, the Diners Club needed to convince a large number of restaurants to accept the new card in order to get the salesmen to sign up. The first Diners Club credit cards were given out in 1950 to 200 people (most were friends and acquaintances of Frank McNamara, a founding partner) and accepted by 14 restaurants in New York. The cards were paper with the accepting locations printed on the back.

In the beginning progress was difficult. Merchants didn't want to pay the Diners Club fee and didn't want competition for their own store cards. Customers didn't want to sign up unless there were a large number of merchants that accepted the card. Nonetheless, by the end of 1950, 20,000 people were using the credit card.

Diners Club continued to grow and by the second year was making a profit ($60,000), but McNamara thought the concept was just a fad and sold his shares in the company to his two partners in 1952 for more than $200,000.

It continued to grow more popular and didn't have competition until 1958. In that year both American Express and the BankAmericard arrived. Until BankAmericard all credit card bills had to be paid in full every month.

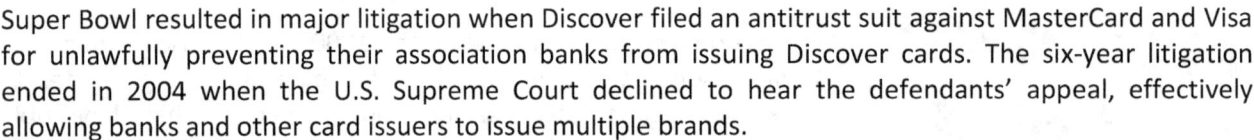

In 1966 BankAmericard went national to become the first licensed general-purpose credit card in the US. It was renamed Visa a decade later to acknowledge its growing international presence.

Also in 1966, a group of California banks formed the Interbank Card Association (ITC), which would soon issue the nation's second major bank card, MasterCard.

The debut of the Sears Corporation's Discover Card at the 1986 Super Bowl resulted in major litigation when Discover filed an antitrust suit against MasterCard and Visa for unlawfully preventing their association banks from issuing Discover cards. The six-year litigation ended in 2004 when the U.S. Supreme Court declined to hear the defendants' appeal, effectively allowing banks and other card issuers to issue multiple brands.

Canada also initially saw banks issue either MasterCard or Visa but that changed in November 2008 when the Competition Bureau issued its new view on duality (see Duality comes to Canada, this chapter).

Credit cards go high tech

Credit cards evolved with the introduction of magnetic (mag) stripe technology. Although magnetic storage was known since World War II and computer data storage from the 1950s, mag wasn't added to credit cards until 1969.

Mag stripe was a wonderful invention, but it was invented in a "safer" world. Used on both credit and debit cards, it was designed to link us to something we wanted to have or do, such as access the funds in our bank account via an ATM or draw on a line of credit through the use of a credit card.

Unfortunately it was not designed to, and was not capable of, stopping other people from copying it and impersonating us in order to use those privileges.

To increase security additional methods such as the use of PINs and neural networks were added, but after 50 years mag stripe could no longer withstand attacks. The internet itself played a role in making it easy for fraudsters to attack magnetic stripe payment cards in volume.

At the end of its lifecycle the counterfeiting of mag stripe resulted in costs and inconvenience to issuers, consumers and merchants. Raising the bar meant adding a secure chip to payment cards – a lengthy and expensive move when you consider that it had to be global.

Cheque this...

On the cheque (check) side, they were processed manually before the mid-1940s.

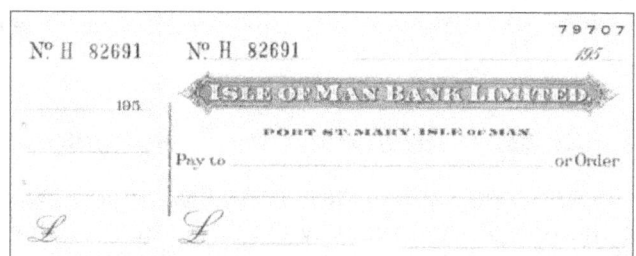

As the number of cheques increased finding an automated way to process them became critical. By the mid-1950s the Stanford Research Institute and General Electric Computer Laboratory had developed the first automated system to process cheques—MICR - Magnetic Ink Character Recognition.

> ***Then the computer revolutionized payment***

Debit Cards and ATMs

The first ATM was deployed by Barclays in London in 1967 and in the US by the Chemical Bank in Long Island, New York, in 1969. The Canadian Imperial Bank of Commerce (CIBC) unveiled the first Canadian ATM, called a "24 hour cash dispenser" Dec. 1, 1969, giving Canadians 24 hour a day access to cash. In 1972 Lloyds Bank issued the first bank card to feature a magnetic strip that used a personal identification number (PIN) for security. Prior to that Barclays matched cheques using carbon 14 to the PIN assigned to the customer.

Hard as it is to imagine now, ATMs were revolutionary. For the first time cash was available in Canada outside of banking hours! The most you could withdraw in a single transaction was $30, but none-the-less it changed the way we banked. The first Canadian card-based ATM network was launched by Credit Unions in Saskatchewan and Alberta in June 1977.

Over time Canadians wanted to withdraw cash from the closest ATM, and because that often meant using another bank's device, a network was needed. In 1984 five financial institutions decided to connect their own Automated Banking Machine networks to give customers broader access to cash. The network was launched through the non-profit Interac Association, a cooperative venture between RBC, CIBC, Scotiabank, TD and Desjardins. In 1986 the first Shared Cash Dispensing (SCD) transaction took place. By 2010 there were over 80 Interac member organizations.

By 1990 many Canadians wanted to skip the step of taking cash from their accounts and use their debit cards to pay at the point of sale, with the funds being transferred from their account to the merchant. Interac Direct Payment (IDP) debuted in the Ottawa region. By 1994 it was available throughout

Canada. The next step was to offer cash back to shoppers when they paid with their debit card, effectively turning the point of sale into a form of ATM.

Today Canadians use both credit and debit cards to pay for online purchases and Interac for many person-to-person (P2P) payments.

As new opportunities emerged it became clear that stakeholders needed a way to communicate and work together to overcome barriers and advance the market.

A new association emerges – changing the payment landscape

It all started in 1989. It was Crystal City, Virginia, where a group of conference delegates met in the bar at the end of the day. They talked about the value of being at a conference where they could learn about security and technology, see new technologies and discuss their ideas with fellow delegates. "We should do something like this in Canada" said one of them, and that was the genesis of ACT Canada.

They came back to Toronto and one of the group, Lorne Boates, took an early retirement from the provincial government to become the first executive director. They hired a management company and a newspaper editor. They adopted bylaws from one of their children's soccer league, and in March 1989 ACT Canada was federally incorporated. Key issuers and suppliers provided seed money.

The founding fathers didn't know what they wanted the association to be but they were sure that they didn't want it to be an industry association. They set out a number of goals around the promotion of what was then called smart card technology (now called chip) and would go on to provide stakeholders the much needed lines of communication to overcome barriers and advance their goals.

At that time smart cards were capable of running multiple applications in the same way that PCs could, unlike magnetic stripe credit and debit cards capable of only a single application. Multi-app was considered to be the promising future for payment and secure ID. Imagine one card capable of transacting both credit and debit, as well as perhaps prepaid, foreign currency and loyalty. Then imagine the dismay of the ACT Canada board when they invited Roland Moreno (known as the inventor of smart cards) to speak at their conference where he told the audience not to try to implement multiple applications because it was too hard.

Within a year a recession hit North America and the association membership plummeted to 18 members and an annual cash flow of $13,000, with $12,000 contractually owed to the bookkeeper. One would have thought that they would close their doors. Actually, it went into hibernation. The executive director retired, the management company and newsletter editor were let go as their contracts expired and the president and past president continued to keep the association alive by publishing a monthly newsletter. After six months they decided that bears hibernate but associations either grow or die - so they resolved to grow it.

It wasn't until much later that ACT Canada finally determined what it was meant to be. The need for a stakeholder association became evident in the areas of payment and secure identification. From that time forward acquirers, issuers, governments, merchants, payment networks, regulators and suppliers came together through ACT Canada to better filter the truth from noise in the marketplace, understand complex issues and facilitate problem resolution.

Ironically, key people within the industry often didn't know each other, but ACT Canada was able to change that as the first payment stakeholder association!

Chip – a slow road to acceptance

Like DVD technology, chip has taken a long time to get to a mass market. Early patents were filed in 1967 and 1968 by Helmut Gröttrup and Jürgen Dethloff. In 1970 Dr Kunitaka Arimura filed the first basic smart card patent in Tokyo, for Japan only. Roland Moreno invented and patented the memory card concept and in 1974 filed the first broad based smart card patents in France and major industrial countries worldwide. Jürgen Dethloff (1976) filed a patent for smart cards with a microprocessor and memory. In 1977 Michel Ugon invented the first microprocessor smart card with two chips: one microprocessor and one memory, and in 1978 he patented the self-programmable one-chip microcomputer (SPOM).

Although the technology found niche applications around the world, it wasn't until card fraud in France became a costly problem in 1992 that it was embraced by the financial sector. Since the 1990s smart cards have also been the subscriber identity modules (SIMs) used in mobile-phone equipment. They also found a home in TV descramblers.

As the French smart cards were seen to be effective in dealing with fraud, talks started between Europay, MasterCard and Visa regarding a global use of chip. Consequently the EMV standards were developed. The first version was published in 1995. That same year the Canadian Chip Card Committee IMV specifications were created. Members of Interac, MasterCard and Visa formed a committee to develop common standards and specifications which would support the introduction of chip cards in Canada.

By 2000 multi-application cards allowed for stronger business cases and a market rush to e-commerce drove use. American Express had 15,000 requests a month for their Amex Blue (chip) Card.

In 2003 Visa Canada announced a move to EMV; followed by Interac, MasterCard and American Express. Interac mandated the move and the others shifted liability - 35 years after the first patents were filed for chip cards.

Stored value

In 1994 Bell Canada introduced a prepaid payphone card named QuickChange, saving callers from Ontario's 416 and 905 exchanges from having to carry quarters to use in payphones. By 1996 this chip based card was popular, but the arrival of cell phones led to the decline of payphones and subsequently the cards.

Nonetheless, the stored value concept caught on. Exact, Mondex and Visa Cash were all bank issued cards in Canada that could be reloaded and used at any participating merchant. All had been developed in other countries and were trialed in Canada in 1996. At that time the cost of cards and infrastructure doomed the business case, but the concept is solid and electronic cash is likely to re-emerge.

Mondex, Visa Cash, Exact and Dexit

Mondex was a smart card electronic cash system; implemented as a stored-value card.

It was conceived by Tim Jones and Graham Higgins of the National Westminster Bank in the United Kingdom. The system was initially developed between 1990 and 1993, with internal trials carried out by approximately 6,000 London-based NatWest staff from 1992. Mondex was publicly unveiled in December 1993.

Initial public trials were carried out from July 1995 by the newly incorporated Mondex International in Swindon, Wiltshire. The public phase required the development and manufacture of numerous merchant devices and smart cards. BT, NatWest and the Midland Bank sponsored and installed retail terminals at car parks, payphones, buses and 700 merchants in the town, and issued Mondex cards to residents.

Mondex launched in a number of markets during the 1990s, expanding from the original trial in Swindon to Hong Kong, New York, and Sherbrooke and Guelph in Canada. MasterCard International, already owning 49%, bought Mondex in 2001.

Dexit offered a rechargeable, contactless, stored-value RFID smart key tag used for electronic payment in on-line or off-line systems when it launched in Toronto in 2003. Funds were transferred from the customer's bank account to a Dexit account, but there was no link to access the account from the key tag to guard against the abuse of lost tags. Dexit accounts could be filled up from the Dexit website, by telephone, at participating merchants, or through pre-approved bank account or credit card balance transfers. It stopped operating in 2006.

Scotiabank and Visa launched a trial of Visa Cash in Barrie, Ontario, in September 1977. It went beyond a reloadable payment card with software built into each card's embedded microchip that could recognize individual merchants, track purchases made at their establishments and respond to pre-set commands like 'Give this user a free xxx for every $xx spent.' The card also supported payment for transit. Cards were not personalized and carried no personal data, emulating cash. Visa Cash in Barrie was still running in 2004.

Exact (as in exact change), a system based on the Belgium Banksys' Proton electronic purse system was trialed in Kingston, Ontario with the Bank of Montreal, Canada Trust and Toronto Dominion (TD) Bank.

In 1997 the stored value experiments in Canada took a turn. A number of Canada's biggest financial institutions decided to join Mondex. Bank of Montreal, Canada Trust, TD Bank, Le Mouvement des caisses Desjardins and National Bank of Canada joined with Canadian Imperial Bank of Commerce (CIBC), Royal Bank, Credit Union Central of Canada and Hong Kong Bank as members of Mondex Canada.

In spite of the issuing clout represented by these FIs, Mondex was ahead of its time and did not roll out nationally. Although it is questionable as to whether it could re-emerge as a card or mobile app in the future, there is no doubt that some of the concepts and processes will come back to advance payment.

The move to EMV

As was the case with many other countries, Canada could not justify the expensive move to EMV based solely on domestic fraud. Our earlier fraud containment steps, such as the use of neural networks, had been significantly successful, but that's not to say that fraud wasn't growing. Added to that problem was the costly migration of fraud from countries that had, or were, converting to EMV.

As Canada determined how long our conversion would take and projected what our fraud losses would be by then, there was a positive business case. This was bolstered by the concern that the US could move before us and any fraud migrating from there would be ruinous.

The first announcement was made in 2003 by Visa, followed by MasterCard, Interac and American Express. In Canada the liability shift was a 3 party model. Put simply, after shift dates the issuer, acquirer or merchant who could not process the transaction on chip assumed the cost of the fraud - if that fraud would have been prevented by the use of chip. Some exceptions existed. Pay at the pump liability shift dates were further out.

Interac debit took a different approach. All Interac transactions had to be executed on chip after 2012 at the ATM and 2015 at the POS. After that Interac debit could not be transacted on magnetic stripe in Canada.

It should be noted that liability rules are complex and the above does not fully cover them.

It was a mammoth undertaking. In addition to the payment networks, stakeholders included issuers, acquirers, merchants, suppliers, regulators, consumers and law enforcement. EMV conversion is not just a technology, fraud or security issue; although all three are a part of it. A successful EMV undertaking is also a stakeholder management exercise.

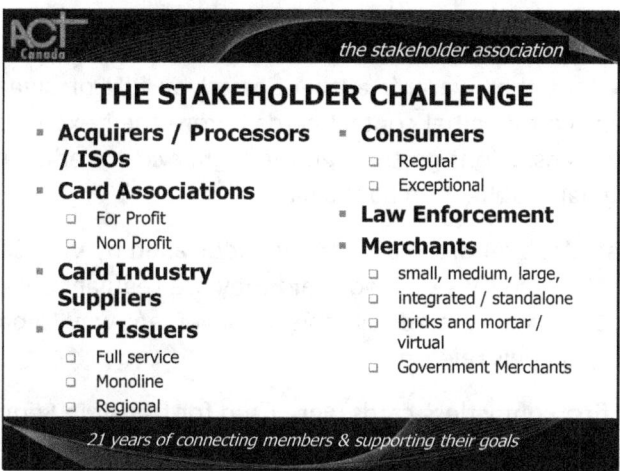

It was not EMV or Chip and PIN that changed so many things for stakeholders, it was moving away from the mag stripe process that had been in place for decades. The same could be said if we were talking about mobile or contactless. Before chip was introduced issuers could put out countless new card products but virtually nothing changed at the point of sale, so there was no need for issuers, merchants and acquirers/processors to discuss technology or processes. That changed with chip and EMV.

Originally stakeholders thought that EMV would come with a checklist of things to be done and you were finished when you had ticked all the boxes. The thought that there would be options didn't occur to people because mag stripe didn't have any.

The next revelation was that the options picked by one stakeholder could impact another. It was like a car company deciding on a design that requires smaller tires than exist in the market and not telling tire manufacturers.

Suddenly it was important to discuss plans with others. That didn't always happen, sometimes resulting in issues that had to be fixed later. Those fixes were often expensive and delayed implementations.

Added to the overall complexity was the fact that many of the stakeholder groups had subgroups with varying requirements, and people within each organization who needed to understand what EMV means in context; marketing, HR, supply management, training and others.

In spite of this the national rollout went well, due in large part to a market trial conducted in Kitchener / Waterloo from October 2007 to October 2008.

Without question chip changed everything and opened the door for new form factors, consumer applications and levels of security.

Duality comes to Canada

Initially Canadian financial institutions chose to issue either MasterCard or Visa products. This remained the custom until 2008. "The Competition Commissioner has formally announced that the Competition Bureau will no longer oppose duality of membership in credit card networks that operate in Canada." This announcement was made in a letter issued in November 2008 to Canada's major credit card issuing banks and financial institutions, credit card networks and other interested parties.

Contactless and new payment forms

Initially it looked as though contactless cards would benefit consumers and merchants because they could speed up payment at the cash register. Issuers seemed to lose because they were taking liability for fraud on some transactions that weren't authenticated by PIN or signature. Not only that, but Canadian issuers paid to replace the initial contact cards before their expiry dates. In reality, issuers did benefit because contactless transactions go through the higher cost credit card networks, resulting in a higher merchant service fee paid to the merchant's bank.

In March 2018 Digital Transactions reported on a study undertaken by Visa Canada. 52% of 1,000 adults polled in February for Toronto-based Visa Canada said they are regular users of contactless cards. Also, 80% of respondents said they view such cards as "a very convenient way to pay" and 45% consider them very secure, according to a Visa news release.

This was 23 years after the first contactless cards were used for transit in Seoul, Korea and 13 years after American Express, MasterCard, Visa, UnionPay, JCB, RuPay and Discover started to launch contactless cards in 2005. Contactless payment was demonstrated at ACT Canada's Cardware conference that same year. Bank of Montreal added contactless to their Mosaik card in 2007 and other financial institutions followed.

In October 2018 Digital Transactions quoted Visa chief executive Alfred F. Kelly as saying, "On the issuing side, several of our largest clients will begin issuing contactless cards over the next few quarters. We expect that there will be over 100 million Visa contactless cards issued in the United States by the end of 2019." If so, contactless cards would represent nearly 12% of Visa's U.S. card base of 856 million as of June 30, based on the latest figures available. That figure includes 521 million debit cards and 335 million credit cards.

In Canada, the chicken and egg (card and reader) scenario was resolved when Ingenico Canada decided to introduce EMV POS readers that could accept both contact and contactless transactions. Because they didn't cost more than contact only, merchants readily bought them, prompting issuers to add contactless capability to their cards.

Statistics should always be looked at from both sides. While 52% of Canadians are regular users of contactless payment, it is equally true to say that 48% of Canadians still aren't after 11 years. That is not a negative comment but another example of how long it takes for technology to find mass acceptance.

The same article states that the polled Canadians are less sure about other payment methods, particularly regarding security. Just 35% of respondents consider digital wallets very secure, followed by mobile apps at 34%, peer-to-peer Web sites at 27% and wearables-based payments at 26%.

On a related note, Digital Transactions finds that only a small minority of consumers regularly use these new payment forms—mobile apps, 9%; digital wallets, 6%; peer-to-peer apps, 4%; or wearables, 3%.

What is interesting is that the payment sector has long believed that Canadians will forego an amount of security in favour of convenience. In the examples above the technology has much the same consumer protection as contact cards, but the perception that they don't cause many Canadians to avoid their use.

The takeaway is that security and privacy should be as important as any other feature when you are marketing a payment product.

Mobile – a cautionary tale

In the late 1980s cell (mobile) phones became popular and it was often predicted that they would be a leapfrog technology, with payment going from mag stripe cards straight to cell phones and bypassing chip cards. Visionaries claimed that consumers would stop carrying real wallets, using digital ones instead. It is now 30 years later and according to a recent study by Ipsos, only 7% of the study group said they had made an NFC mobile payment in 2017. The two major things holding back mobile payment are security concerns (perceived) and apathy.

The first – security – could be fixed quickly if the industry broadly educated consumers on the safety afforded them when they use mobile payment. The second is harder to fix. After many digital wallet issuers claimed that physical wallets were no longer necessary, consumers felt mislead because they still needed something for government issued ID and private sector papers such as insurance slips. Without the benefit of being able to abandon wallets consumers felt that cards were as good as phones for payment and more secure. Ironically, consumers do use mobile phone for shopping; to read reviews, check competitors' pricing, confirm stock availability, and even take a picture of the goods they are considering buying. Then they most often use a card to make the payment.

The two takeaways that should be considered with any innovation are:

✓ make consumers comfortable with your security (and privacy if personal data is involved)
✓ give them something better, not just different

Payment and chip milestones of the past 40 years

By the year 2000, Canadians were using smart (chip) cards for stored value and e-cash, loyalty programs, transit, telecommunications, physical access, time and attendance tracking, electronic gift certificates, golf and health care.

1984	Five financial institutions decide to link their own Automated Banking Machine (ABM) networks to give customers broader access to cash dispensing
1986	The first Shared Cash Dispensing (SCD) transaction takes place
	Royal Bank uses smart cards as part of electronic cash management services for larger corporate customers
1989	Royal Bank pilots multi-function chip cards in an internal staff pilot (1500 cards)
1990s	Mondex, Exact, Visa Cash – enter the Canadian market
1990	CIBC rolls out multi-function cards in an internal staff pilot
	Interac Direct Payment (IDP) debuts in the capital region
1992	Greenshield Insurance Company pilots portable drug records for subscribers and to enable claim payments
	City of Montreal uses smart cards to enable flex time for 1100 union and non-union workers
	Montreal Transit's smart card project is the first open to the general public, essentially electronic passports for Transit '92
1994	IDP becomes available nationally
1996	First EMV standards are published
1997	Mobil launches their contactless payment system, Speedpass, allowing users to pay for gas with a key fob pre-loaded with cash at participating gas stations
2003	Visa Canada announces their move to EMV, followed by Interac, MasterCard and American Express
	Interac mandates the move and the others shift liability
2008	Competition Commissioner formally announces that the Competition Bureau will no longer oppose duality of membership in credit card networks that operate in Canada
2010	CIBC is the first bank in Canada to deliver a mobile banking app
2011	QuickTap, PayPass, PayWave, Google Wallet, and Android Pay enter the market
	Barclay and Orange launch Europe's first mobile wallet: QuickTap, allowing customers to pre-load their phones and pay.
	MasterCard PayPass and Visa payWave are born
	Google launches Google Wallet, allowing users to pay with their mobile phones at participating retailers
	Android Pay allows users to make purchases with their Android devices via NFC
2015	EMV in the U.S. One of the later markets to adopt it, the U.S. implements EMV, prompting thousands of merchants to switch over to NFC-capable terminals that enable contactless payments
2016	Apple finally reaches an agreement with Canada's five major banks

Note: the above milestones are just some of many payment advancements made in Canada and around the world.

Classic hits, misses and lessons to be learned

Let's take a look at three innovations that had tremendous potential but failed to live up to initial expectations. In each case some early assumptions were correct and others were wrong.

The number of assumptions they got wrong could have been far fewer if more questions had been asked in the early stages. It takes time and discipline to ask questions when you are worried that your competitor may get to the finish line first, but at a time when far more than 50% of innovations fail, answers to those questions will help you decide whether the finish line is over the edge of the cliff!

Dot.com

In the late 1990s, it was forecast that many companies would abandon bricks and mortar to sell solely on the internet. Early predictions were that we would use our TVs to surf the net and make purchases. In the end it was the gold-rush all over again, with a few getting rich and most losing their "stakes".

What problem does it solve?	In theory, online sales eliminate many of the costs associated with brick and mortar stores and those savings can be passed on to the customer who is able to shop from the convenience of home or office (or on-the-go once smartphones entered the market)
What they got right ✓	There is a significant market for online sales
What they got wrong ✗	<ul><li>**The timeline**. It took more than 10 years for online purchases to take off. Christmas gift buying started the trend and it took more years - and Amazon - to take it to an everyday way of buying.</li><li>The impact on bricks and mortar. While new companies such as Amazon went directly to online selling, traditional merchants kept their retail stores and added internet purchasing. In 2018 Amazon and other e-tailers started to experiment with physical locations.</li><li>No-one was willing to give up TV programs to surf the net on their TVs</li></ul>
Who made money?	Start-up founders who had successful IPOs, web designers and a few e-tailers. The stock market, office suppliers, computer vendors and other suppliers initially made money supporting start-ups, but then lost as clients went under.
Who lost money?	Many venture capitalists and investors as well as employees of failed start-ups
Lessons to be learned	<ul><li>Consumers want options on where, how and when they buy</li><li>Solid business plans are important. Investors didn't look for them but bought into the market noise - rushing to get to the market first and investing in anything with dotcom in its name</li><li>Online has to offer consumers more than their bricks and mortar competitors. It could be price, convenience, experience or a combination</li><li>Consumer habits take a long time to change</li><li>Once again, the market growth projections were dangerously off in terms of how quickly the market would grow to a profitable state</li></ul>

Mobile commerce

Of our three innovations this is the one that currently has the greatest potential, but it also has a 20 year history of missteps and slow growth. More than any other payment technology, mobile was driven by what it could do as opposed to what consumers wanted it to do. That is finally changing.

What problem does it solve?	It allows consumers to shop online when they are away from their desktop PCs and tablets.
What they got right ✓	Consumers will use mobile phones to shop if it is easy, affordable and secure
What they got wrong ✗	That : ▪ The age of the consumer would not be relevant to adoption rates (studies show that age, gender and market all impact the rate) ▪ The Asian market was proof that other markets would follow similar adoption rates and trends (in many Asian families, smartphones are the only internet connected devices) ▪ Mobile network operators would rent space on their SIM cards to financial institutions for payment apps (with both stakeholders adding on costs, this approach was too expensive for the end-user) ▪ Consumers would carry digital wallets and no longer need physical wallets (this has been more successful with Gen X users and less with seniors and baby boomers) ▪ Consumers would prefer to pay using their phone rather than their card. A 2018 JP Morgan Chase study found that while 56% of large businesses and 25% of small businesses said they accept mobile wallets, only 16% of consumers said they had ever used a mobile wallet. ▪ Consumers would pick convenience over security (numerous studies show that security and lack of ubiquity are the most prevalent reasons that consumers don't use digital wallets at this point) ▪ Consumers would use their phones, not desktops or laptops for m-commerce (mobile phones are used more often in the morning, desktops throughout the day and tablets in the evening – most likely indicating the devices available to consumers throughout the day) ▪ **And the timeline.** By 1997 people were forecasting that credit and debit cards would disappear and "cell" phones would take their place.
Who made money?	▪ E-tailers offering products and/or services that were more attractive than bricks and mortar retailers (price, variety, no-cost shipping, easy returns etc.)
Who lost money?	▪ Early market entrants and investors
Lessons to be learned	▪ Adoption is influenced by user's age, gender, income and culture, perceived security and privacy concerns, ease of use and ubiquity of participating merchants ▪ A solid business case is more important than an early-to-market strategy ▪ Those who enter the market later can learn from the mistakes of earlier entrants, but being too late is as bad as being too early. Knowing when and where to enter a market is critically important. ▪ The greater the number of stakeholders in the ecosystem, the greater the complexity, increasing time to reach market acceptance and profit.

Crypto currency, blockchain and digital currency

The first two have been the brightest shiny objects of the past 5 years. While sometimes considered to be the same thing they are not. The third, digital currency (also called e-cash) is "minted", backed by governments, has all the same attributes as fiat coins and paper bills and is usable online. It also allows the unbanked access to subscription services.

What problem does it solve?	The blockchain process builds trust that a transaction (of any kind) is accurate because a number of people agree that it is. Crypto currency allows digital transmission of funds although it is not the first or only way to do that. It is also said that it is fully anonymous and not susceptible to government control, although both claims are not totally accurate. Digital currency removes the need to get and carry bills and coins and allows "cash" to be spent online with a degree of anonymity.
What they got right ✓	Many people want payment anonymity, but some have not thought about the identifying information needed if a product or service is to be delivered or returned. Many people want funds that they consider to be outside of the control or scrutiny of governments and others want the convenience of a digital currency.
What they got wrong ✕	▪ **The timeline.** Merchants have been slow to accept crypto currencies for several reasons; time to validate a transaction, fluctuation in monetary value, government scrutiny and policies, and cost to convert to "hard" cash ▪ Consumer confidence does drop when Bitcoin and other crypto-currencies are hacked ▪ Terminology. The average person has some understanding of the value of their country's currency and what influences that value. Crypto currency is a misleading term because it can delude people into thinking that it is backed by a government and has some semblance of stability. In reality, it is less like a currency and more like dealing in futures.
Who made money?	▪ Unfortunately crypto currencies are the payment method of choice for scammers, so they have benefited as the value of individual coins rise. ▪ It could be said that the miners – the people who do the work to agree that a transaction is accurate – make money, but they have offsetting costs related to computing and the time they have to spend to reach consensus ▪ Investors, when the value of crypto currency increased
Who lost money?	▪ Investors, when the value dropped ▪ Users, when wallets were hacked or exchanges went under
Lessons to be learned	▪ Governments are not in favour of unregulated currencies entering their market ▪ Consumers want to be able to spend their funds everywhere they shop and crypto currencies are still not accepted broadly ▪ Blockchain processing is not infallible

The Payments Road Map

We've looked at the history of payment so it's time to look at where we are and where we're going. As I have often said, "payment is not for the faint of heart". This chapter looks at the players, issues and opportunities. Market roadmaps rarely show dead-ends but this chapter will give you tools to help you avoid them by outlining the difference between winners and losers and providing tips to identify them before it is too late.

What is driving change?

Canada and much of the world invested heavily in EMV to curb card counterfeiting and provide a foundation for additional security measures.

 When you look back at the history of payment, whenever security investments are made they are followed by new investments in products and services that might drive revenue / profit.

Payment as a concept is independent of technology, but in the past we limited ourselves through the use of plastic cards and magnetic stripes! That meant there was very little change at the point of sale but chip changes that. The same (secure) chips we deployed for EMV already enable most of the innovation we've talked about for the past 10 years and will fuel many more over the next 20, empowering more choices for issuers, merchants and consumers.

Chip is the first technology to put a fully functioning computer into a consumer's wallet and that computer functions as an active partner in providing security. Chip security itself has evolved over the years to meet increasingly stronger attacks and has the capability to continue to evolve.

Technology and payments: evolutionary or revolutionary?

It is often said that the pace of technological change keeps speeding up. In a survey of 1409 chief executives around the world (PWC Global CEO survey 2016) those in the financial sector named 3 things as extremely concerning:

- overregulation (57%)
- cyber-threats (38%)
- *speed of technological change (37%)*

I can never quite decide whether time is flying by or just crawling. In payment, things seem to change so quickly. Just think about what has entered the market in the past few years. HCE, IoT, TEE, P2PE, DCC, AI and I suspect a lot of other acronyms. There's contactless, blockchain, faster payments, biometric authentication, social media and more.

The technology that supports much of this innovation has been around for years but we were focussed on EMV and other things, so it all sat in the pipeline. When we were ready to look at investments that would drive revenue and profit there was a lot of technology to consider.

On the other hand it seems that some things have taken a long time. DVDs are based on a technology invented before World War 2. It first came to market called optical disc, designed to let companies and governments store and retrieve a lot of information quickly. It was a viable use for the technology but that market wasn't very profitable. It resurfaced as CDs with music. Bingo – that was profitable. Then it morphed into DVDs for movies. Over 80 years have passed since the technology was invented, but it wasn't until 1982 that it found its market when Abba's "The Visitor" was released on CD.

In 1992 Cartes Bancaire converted their payment cards to chip 35 years after the technology was first invented. Now, 26 years later, we are still waiting for the US and China to finish their EMV conversions. It wasn't until fraud became an uncontrollable problem that the financial sector moved from mag stripe to chip.

Mobile commerce, by these standards, is on track. There are claims that the first mobile phone was developed in 1908 (yes – 1908) but realistically it can be said that the first handheld came out in 1973. It has found many profitable uses ranging from enabling mobile phone calls, to cameras, to internet browsers. When it finds a niche for payment in the market, one that drives profitable revenue, it too will perceived as "flying" into the market.

 Does it always take 50 years or more for a technology to live up to its potential? Definitely not. Every technology can get there as soon as someone figures out how to use it to make money. So when people ask you to invest in something, they better be able to tell you how it will make money and when!

Knowing the difference between evolutionary and revolutionary change and its nuances can impact your career. The responsible thing to do is to look at the bright shiny objects that could impact your organization, but that look should be clinical, not passionate. It involves asking and answering many questions so that you can determine how much to invest and when to invest it. Unbridled passion leads to investing too much, too early.

There are those who would argue that all innovation needs to be adopted often out of fear that competitors will. This approach has led to the growing number of people in payment who say they are stressed by the pace that new technology enters the market, and yet, we control that pace.

Very little technology is revolutionary. Most bright shiny objects are actually evolutionary and it isn't until each one solves a problem that customers embrace it. The technology we use today for USB fobs was invented before World War II – in other words, before 1939. Between the 1930s and 1980s, some investors won and others lost.

 Payment is complex and rarely benefits from revolutionary approaches. Evolution allows you to course correct to find the balance between your goals and your customers' expectations.

Chip: putting payment on the road to the future

 Chip solved many of the pain points of mag stripe by being highly counterfeit resistant. Its suite of options allows you to layer protection to meet the needs of individual applications or transactions. That reassures investors that the technology has a long future for enabling new functions, applications, interfaces and form factors. Although today's chips can handle multiple applications that can be downloaded after the chip is issued, it is unclear as to whether smartphones have taken over this space from cards. Likely it has, but there may be niche applications where a card is preferable to a phone, for example in some security applications.

Business cases change because chip attracts new "issuers" such as telecommunication carriers (MNOs) and third parties. Liability can change. You are dealing with all the capabilities and complexities of a computer, unlike the small piece of static data that mag stripe could handle.

Even though we're used to having chips on our payment cards and in our mobile phones, it is worth pointing out that these differ from most of those in our computers because they are highly secure. The software, firmware and manufacturing security, along with the computing power within the chip, are all used to protect data and transactions.

It is fair to say that chip revolutionized payment; enabling mobile payment, wearables, IoT and applications that will come in the future. This technology has been around since 1969, moved into the mainstream of payments in1993, but as the following statistics show, we are still only half way towards securing all payment cards with chip.

As of April 2018, EMVCo reported that aggregated data (published by EMVCo) shows that by the end of 2017 54.6% of all cards issued globally were EMV® -enabled. The number of EMV payment cards in worldwide circulation increased by 1 billion over the previous 12 months to a total of 7.1 billion.

The data demonstrates that 63.7% of all card-present transactions conducted across the world between January and December 2017 used EMV chip technology, increasing from 52.4% in 2016.

Change takes time!

Stakeholders: both an ongoing challenge and opportunity

Stakeholder engagement and management became necessary with the advent of chip and are now an ongoing part of the roadmap.

Who are the payment stakeholders today and will they change as we move forward? This is a trick question. Some people would like to make this far more complicated, but beware. Complexity sometimes opens loopholes.

Payment stakeholders are those who:

- accept payment; people, consumers, merchants, businesses, governments
- make payments; people, consumers, merchants, businesses, governments
- facilitate payments; financial institutions, payment networks, acquirers, processors, gateways, etc.
- regulate payments; governments and government agencies and
- those who supply products and services to support payments (a very big, big group)

Anyone who says they are a payment stakeholder falls into one of these five groups. But wait... (here's the trick), there are two more groups; bad guys and law enforcement. The first is often well funded and willing to invest in human resources and technology to take other people's money and information. The second is usually underfunded, has less technology and deals with the societal heartache when bad guys mess with payment and identity.

What do these stakeholders want? Well, 6 out of 7 have always wanted, and always will want, a safe, secure, reliable, scalable, ubiquitous, affordable and usable payment process. You might notice that I didn't say convenient. More on that in the next chapter.

The Predictable Future of Payment

At a high level, certain patterns have been in place since the cavemen and most change has been evolutionary. Periodically new technologies emerge and change many parts of our lives, including payment. Computers, the internet, smartphones and secure chip are the most notable and they will continue to enable future payment innovations.

As technology changes so do people's wants and fears, but their expectations change more slowly. By studying all three, you can predict the future.

The crystal ball shows that everyone wants payment that is affordable, consistently easy to use, secure and available everywhere they want to transact.

What will drive future change?

That may be a trick question. There will always be new technologies and companies willing to invest in research, pilots and even rollouts. They may want to be seen by customers and shareholders as innovative, or they may do it simply to force their competitors to make similar investments.

Some change will be driven by criminals who invest in technology and human resources so that they can profitably attack us. Because of them we will continuously upgrade our security.

Other change, the most profitable and enduring change, is driven by customers who are willing to pay. Apple, Google, Amazon and Blackberry are all examples of companies that offered new products and services that consumers wanted; even though they didn't know it before they saw it.

Chip itself is a technology that will support decades of change.

What products and services will consumers want?

- The person to person (P2P) market is poised for growth.
- The desire for payment ubiquity now extends to electronic cash. It must meet the criteria of physical cash including being "minted" and backed by governments and supporting anonymity of use. It also provides access to subscription services for the unbanked.
- The convenience of having payment embedded in apps they already use.
- Travelers would like dynamic currency conversion and the same payment experience they have at home.
- Consumers would like instant redemption of loyalty points.
- Generally, products that offer more convenience without diminishing privacy or security .

The question is whether issuers and innovators will "see a need, fill a need" or create a need in the mind of the consumer with breakthrough marketing as did PayPal, Apple, Google and Blackberry.

What will consumers expect and assume from payment products?

If you want consumers to buy your payment innovation it has to be better than what they already have, not just different. They will expect:

- multi or omni channel acceptance
- low or no cost transactions
- privacy and security and

- the same level of regulated protection from all participants!

Even then, don't expect that adoption will be quick.

Who pays?

Consumers have shown a willingness to pay for anything they want; premium credit cards, mobile phones, specialized coffees and many more things that would have been inconceivable fifteen years ago.

Other stakeholders may have reasons to pay for innovation such as drawing customers away from competitors, pressing competitors to make investments before they are ready, or avoiding a penalty such as fraud.

How do consumers feel about security and convenience?

Online merchants are reporting that consumers want to "feel friction" when they're paying electronically and can abandon their purchases when they believe that there's not enough security tied to the transaction. This contradicts the belief that consumers will choose convenience over security. That may have been the case in the early days of the internet, but data breeches and payment fraud have increased consumer concerns. Studies from 2017 and 2018 confirm that consumers expect and welcome the need to authenticate themselves when making a payment.

Nearly 6 in 10 consumers pay bills on line but half of them have concerns about the security of doing so, according to "Expectations & Experiences: Consumer Payments", a 2018 consumer survey from Fiserv Inc.

And although consumers are interested in new payment features and functionalities, nearly half (46 percent) are confused by the assortment of financial products and services available.

The report also finds that:

- 53% of consumers say they like to be connected to the internet at all times, but 53% also say they strongly distrust internet security or privacy
- of those who have not used mobile banking in the past 30 days, 57% cited security as the main reason
- at 24%, security is of less concern with person-to-person payments, ranked behind their preference for other payments methods (44%) and unwillingness to pay a fee (38%).

In another study, consumer concerns about data security and privacy are reportedly hampering the move to emerging payments. More than 5,000 consumers were polled for the Paysafe study, "Lost in Transaction: Payment Trends 2018".

- 50% cited fraud as the greatest barrier to using emerging payments; 48% expressed concerns around the use of their data
- 65% thought voice-activated systems are not secure; 63% worried about being overcharged
- 56% reported that checkout-free stores — where smart technologies tally items in the shopping basket and automate payments — sound too risky, or said they'd need to know more before using them

What will it take to make it happen?

A better understanding of what consumers need, want or can be made to want is critical. Figuring that out as well as how best to deliver it involves all of the stakeholders in the chain: acquirers, issuers, merchants, payment networks, regulators, suppliers and, of course, consumers. You would be shocked to learn how often decisions are made without input from these groups.

Winners and losers – what makes the difference?

In this age where immediacy is expected, companies often fail to take the time to ask all the questions that would tell them, with a certain degree of accuracy, whether their plans would succeed in the market. As evidence of this, look at how many innovations either fail to make it to market or fail in market.

The McKinsey & Co. report on "The Future of Digital Wallets" states that historically the failure rate of payment innovations is about 98%. The odds of success certainly are bad, but they can be improved.

Why does failure happen?

- Some of it has to do with unrealistic expectations.
- Some of it is because it takes much longer to introduce most payment products and services than expected, and during that period factors can change and new innovations can be distracting.
- A lot of it is because there is a great deal of competition in the fintech space and many products fail to even make it to market.

So why are we attracted to all these potential products and services? Some of it is explained by how we're first introduced to them. I think of it as "the hype". It's based on the premise that 100% of new technologies / concepts can do something - and that 100% will appeal to a certain group of users.

While that's true, many innovations will be predicted to enjoy rapid growth based on false assumptions. It is these growth projections that often separate winners from losers. Winners tend to know that it takes a long time to reach the mass and profitable stage of a market.

Other factors that often lead to failure are the fear of missing out, which is greater today than I have ever seen it over the past 25 years, and the fear of being disintermediated.

 Winners tend to ask a lot of questions before investing a lot of resources and money!

Recognizing dead ends before it's too late

From "it could" to "it does" takes a LONG time. If your success means selling to a mass market for an extended period, you'll benefit from:

- standards & interoperability
- technology and /or application testing & certification
- ubiquity of acceptance & issuing
- the ability to move beyond the market's early adopters

If the first 3 are not in place, and you don't have a clear plan to achieve number 4, you have a very long road ahead of you. Knowing that, you can either limit your investment or consider the project a dead end until these factors are more favourable.

If, however, everything is in place, there are still dozens of questions that need to be asked and answered. Those answers will clearly identify dead ends before you've committed your resources.

What about recessions?

Although we all dread recessions there is an upside. I've seen planning and strategizing activities go up during each recession since 1980, followed by implementations as the market recovered.

In 20 Years from now...

Patterns and cycles will look much the same as they do today with innovation and adoption rates facing similar challenges and offering comparable opportunities. Undoubtedly payment will remain complex. This is 3D business chess, but by working together with other stakeholders you can plan to succeed.

The Insiders' Secret Weapon

So far we've talked a lot about technology and how it changes payment, but there are other factors that will impact innovation. One currently being reported on is how millennials and Gen Xers prefer to communicate. Millennials have already surpassed Gen Xers as being the most prominently represented generation in the workforce and they would rather text than talk for a number of reasons. This is a new challenge, coming at a time when communication is vital among stakeholders who can impact your success. As a part of each stakeholder group, they need to be drawn into the dialogue.

This chapter looks at how payment market shapers work together to further their goals, both corporate and career. It is about how you can do the same. I called it the insiders' secret weapon because so many people I met in payment either didn't know about the benefits of working with other stakeholders or didn't believe in it. After 27 years of being an insider I know it works.

If you want to go far

There is an old African proverb that says, "If you want to go fast, go alone; if you want to go far, go together. "

It's human nature to want to control your own destiny, but that is not the same thing as working alone. Our fates are influenced by other individuals. Highly successful people accept that and use it to their advantage.

Our ability to succeed is based in large part on the tools we have at our disposal and by how well and willingly we employ them. One of the most effective tools is reaching out to others with similar goals and challenges. Since 1989 payment insiders from around the world have done that through ACT Canada. Members have, and likely will continue to lead the market given their history, expertise and the fact that they work together through the association.

Having access to people who can impact your plans, information and insights – these are the secret weapons that insiders use and ACT Canada provides.

This will become increasingly valuable because payment is getting more complex with:

- AI
- APIs
- Biometric Authentication
- Competitors
- Corporate training requirements
- Customer expectations
- Digital Currency
- EMD - E-Money Directive
- Encryption
- Equipment
- FinTech
- Form factors
- Fraud attacks
- GDPR
- HR requirements
- IoT
- In app payment
- Interoperability issues
- KBA - Knowledge-Based Authentication
- Loyalty
- Marketing directions
- e-commerce versus e-window shopping
- Open banking and PSD2
- Prepaid
- Processes
- Quantum encryption
- Regulations
- Sales channels and omni-channel
- Standards
- Technologies
- Testing requirements
- Tokens
- Wallets
- Wearables
- And others

In addition to all of this there are the challenges of market noise and the fear of missing an opportunity. Payment today is like 3D chess. As we said in the last chapter, "The Future of Digital Wallets" study by McKinsey & Co. states that, "Most payments innovations fail; historically, the failure rate is about 98%." How your career advances depends on what questions about innovation you ask or ignore – and who you ask.

Insiders' secret weapons

Successful people know that there will always be times when competitive interests will drive the agenda, but they are also wise enough to know that many of the things needed to develop a healthy market benefit from collaboration among stakeholders. They work together to build or protect a market in which they can then compete.

The secret is to find a neutral forum where all stakeholder groups can learn, share information and help others understand their own processes, needs and goals. This is a business issue. The dialogue must move beyond technology and look at product and market development, training, human resources, marketing and other strategic business elements.

ACT Canada has been that forum since 1989 for acquirers, issuers, merchants, payment networks, regulators, users, vendors and all parties with a vested interest in payment; giving members access to information, insights, market analysis and other stakeholders.

Given the current complexities of payment, hundreds of questions that should be asked come to mind. Many are the standard questions we ask on all projects, but some of them are new and unique to today's technology. Some are even unique to the sector or organization. There are a lot of reasons why people don't ask questions, but that is for another day and my next book.

The person who is willing to ask questions; the person who carefully prepares those questions to get the best information – that person will have a more successful career. Being a member of ACT Canada connects you to people who can provide answers and even suggest other questions you should ask.

 For the most effective networking, seek out people and organizations that have the broadest connections within your industry. They know people who know people!

Getting the information and insights you need

Insiders are adept at accessing information without wasting time. While they may use all five of the following channels they excel at using the fifth.

1. The internet
   - As a source of information the good thing about the internet is how much information is available - and as the old joke goes – the bad thing about the internet is how much information is available. For example, biometrics: 92,900,000 sites, biometrics in Canada: 9,250,000 and payment biometrics in Canada: 8,410,000 and biometric authentication: 1,320,000.

   - Who has the time to look at more than the top ten or twenty? Even then you have to determine whether each site reflects up-to-date or even accurate information.

2. Email & social media
   - These are great if you know who has the right answer to your question. Otherwise both these channels can be more opinion than fact based.

3. External commissioned research
   - This is a great option if you have sufficient funds, can wait for the answer(s) and have input into the questions and selection of people who will be interviewed.

4. From within your company – institutional memory
   - People change jobs, so don't expect that a company has retained knowledge even though it may have participated in a trial or roll out.

5. Stakeholder Dialogue
   - Talking with others who have a stake in payment has many benefits:

     - ✓ They share many of your same goals and challenges
     - ✓ Information will be in the context of your market
     - ✓ Ideas are shared and differing perspectives are offered when you are with a group. The words, "I hadn't thought of that" or "Now that you say that, it makes me think..." are indicators of value.
     - ✓ Insights can come from a conversation with a colleague or others in a meeting. The more people gathered together to discuss a common interest, the greater the likelihood that you will gain insight. And when you open your world to new people who share your interests, you stand an even better chance of learning from them.
     - ✓ Creative, collaborative thought - the type that happens when someone hears something and responds verbally. You just can't do that in email or text.

 Stakeholder dialogue can be the timeliest and most cost effective tool available to us.

Strategic Leadership Teams

Current and future innovations represent opportunities for the majority of ACT Canada members. Most of the research each does is substantially the same as the others, so the association brings members together to advance their knowledge through strategic leadership teams. By leveraging the team's resources this approach saves members both time and money. (For more information on SLTs and papers they've published see Appendix C.)

Insiders use SLTs to:
- access assistance and expertise
- set direction on priority issues
- influence key market initiatives
- work with others on non-competitive issues
- educate other stakeholders on their processes and/or concerns and propose solutions
- publish widely read thought-leadership papers
- gain in-depth and timely exposure to the industry's best practices
- hear multiple stakeholder perspectives
- achieve personal and professional satisfaction from making a difference and
- network with market shapers

You can join other insiders to profit from insights, networking and visibility through SLTs.

From surviving to thriving: the challenge of emerging markets

As companies try to develop market acceptance for new products or services there can be elephants in the room. Consumers often base their opinion of something new on the first three things they hear about it, so you not only have to build enthusiasm in the market, but often you have to defend it as well.

To ensure market acceptance, you need:

- advocacy and (sometimes) lobbying to build awareness
- market development to inspire enthusiasm and
- issues management to maintain confidence

Although you could do all this on your own, associations are ideally suited to do them on behalf of members.

"Careers – what's in this for you?"

Careers are like houses, built one brick at a time. Usually many tradesmen work on it, each adding their skills and knowledge and all contributing to the final vision of the architect.

In our careers the skilled tradesmen are the people we deal with, whether they are peers, superiors or subordinates. They work in our companies and in others. Sometimes they provide information we need. Other times it is insight, enthusiasm or inspiration.

They challenge our assumptions or ideas. Sometimes they seem to slam doors in our faces forcing us to look for new ways to move ahead. This accounts for some of the hardest, but best, lessons.

All these people help build our careers and contribute to the success of our projects and companies.

Bringing people together to help members achieve their goals is one of ACT Canada's primary purposes. Join ACT, join the dialogue, help your career and help your organization.

Don't underestimate the power of connecting with people and organizations that can favourably impact your success.

Don't undervalue the influence you have when you're able to talk with other stakeholders.

These connections and conversations will lead to insights that can get you to market quicker, drive more revenue and profit, and mitigate risks.

Working together – works!

Insights

As I was researching material for this book I reread the ACT Canada news editorials from 2000 to 2017. Many spoke to market activities of the time, but some dealt with insights that are timeless. Here are my favourite 20 that still speak to the present and the future.

What I learned from Colonel Chris Hadfield

September 2015

The quick answer is "everything you need to know to succeed" no matter what you do for a living or who you work for.

I was really fortunate to hear Colonel Hadfield speak last week. It was one of those life-changing moments, not because he was an astronaut, but because of what he said. He talked about many things but the one that really resonated with me was how to mitigate the risk of dying in space. He pointed out that in less than 9 minutes after liftoff you are either in orbit around the world or you are dead.

From there he talked about how to stay alive when you are living on the space station with a very small team and you can't call 911 in an emergency. He pointed out that every additional skill your team has is an improved chance for success. So if you are in a small team you need people with both specialized and generalized skills and experience. That isn't surprising but his next insight might be, unless you work in risk management.

He said that we shouldn't visualize success but instead we should always ask, as space teams do, "What can kill us next?" In consistently asking and answering that question, they were able to avoid or manage situations that could have killed them, such as the escaping ammonia problem.

This approach is often siloed in most organizations, but it should be pervasive and serve as a pillar of the foundation of every department. Product planning, development, marketing, sales, HR, finance and every other part of your organization should constantly ask, "What could kill us next?" Identifying weaknesses and vulnerabilities and then developing strategies to overcome them in our products and processes is a great way to guarantee success.

It isn't just rocket science, it's corporate. After all, if it is good enough to build a space station and launch rockets, it will work for all of us.

My house - my rules!

February 2015

Remember when your parents said that to you, or perhaps you have said it to your own children. Should it be any different in the workplace? Let's take a look. You want your family to be happy. In your business you want your customers, employees, shareholders and even regulators to be happy. The scale is bigger but the concept is the same.

In your family it takes work to establish and adhere to standards and values. The same is true of the workplace. In both scenarios people have to take individual responsibility and lapses need to be corrected in a way that encourages better future outcomes.

We are at an interesting point in the evolution of payment and even more so related to customer authentication and general issues of ID, data and privacy. Technology is not the factor that will determine who will and won't be successful or profitable. Enough of us have access to technology to make it a somewhat neutral factor. Is the level of education and the skill sets of our employees the differentiator? Not as much as we would like to think. I believe it is an issue of character and judgment.

CEO does not stand for Chief Ethics Officer and every single person in the company is responsible for making choices that support long term relationships and corporate health. People who want to reap quick profits at the expense of long term sustainability should be removed from their positions.

CIO does not stand for Chief Integrity Officer because it is everyone's responsibility to do the right thing. Sometimes that brings short term penalties, but again, everyone needs to protect the long term viability of the company.

The decisions that will be made in this emerging market will likely touch on how our personal data is used. Each of us needs to think through the pros and cons of data usage employing our commitment to ethics and integrity.

And one last one - CFO doesn't stand for Chief Fix It Officer. (I bet you thought I was going in a different direction with the acronym, didn't you) Everyone who takes on a responsibility should fulfil it to the very best of their abilities. Frankly, I'm tired of people who work harder at justifying why they didn't get something done than they would have had to work to succeed. There is no Chief Fix It Officer in your life so do what you committed to or accept that there must be consequences. Please.

Do you know it, think it, or just hope it's true?

April 2015

In 26 years, I have never seen so much doubt and concern how payment is changing. The usual players are present: visionaries, missionaries and nay-sayers.

The missionaries talk passionately. They will tell you definitively how payment will change and what every stakeholder will have to do, or not do. These people are dangerous. I used to be one of them. Nay-sayers will tell you all the reasons why things won't work. They often raise good points and can bring value if you take what they say and then look for solutions and mitigating strategies.

Visionaries combine the best of missionaries and nay-sayers. They identify goals, stages and stakeholders. They focus on how to overcome barriers and they understand both the value and necessity of working with those stakeholders.

Visionaries are the people who successfully innovate, who see how to make things more efficient and profitable. Visionaries provide the competitive edge and enhance the careers and lives of those around them. These heroes are often misunderstood and undervalued. Isn't that strange?

Today's market is being driven by missionaries. They are passionate about where technology could take us. I think they are right that mobile offers much, but they just don't seem to think about what and who it takes to get there. Visionaries know that it takes more than investing money. **Be a visionary!**

Visiting the land of What-If

June 2005

You've heard of this place. It is right next door to the LAND OF CONVENIENCE and also borders on the LAND OF WISHFUL THINKING. Beyond its borders for those who travel far enough is another land - one of progress, rewards and dreams realized. This land, SUCCESS, is the one that we all want to get to, but the road through WHAT IF can be difficult and expensive. Part of the problem is that WHAT IF is unmapped and it has countless roads. On your way to SUCCESS there may be many routes that could get you there, but in WHAT IF they are often twisted and sometimes double back on themselves, so without a map you'll need the courage of your convictions.

On your travels you'll see many signposts, but you better question who put them there and why. Not everyone wants you to reach SUCCESS. Beware those who would tell you to rush ahead before you have decided on your final destination. Beware those who would tell you to hold back because there may be a bigger, better or different "something" further down the road. They would detour you to the LAND OF WISHFUL THINKING. It may be close to SUCCESS but it can't offer you the same advantages. Ignore those from the LAND OF CONVENIENCE who are intellectually lazy and see everything as an "all or nothing" scenario and find the "nothing" option to be the easiest. Most importantly, reject those who stand to profit if they can slow or stop your trip to SUCCESS.

In the context of secure payment, success is reaching your business or policy goals. To get there you'll need access to good information from a variety of sources. Your trip through the land of WHAT IF can be useful, because there you can ask questions that will help you define your goals and develop strategic plans for reaching them. But remember, while it's a nice place to visit, you wouldn't want to stay there.

For Canadians, the road to balancing security, convenience and privacy through the use of cards, mobile phones and wearables, takes us on a complex journey. Information and insights are the pathways that can lead us to SUCCESS.

Death, taxes and...

January 2014

It is said that these are the only certainties in life, but that is far from true. Here are three more: options, choices and outcomes. Not a day goes by that we don't have all three of these and how you deal with them influences the course of your life.

My grandmother and I used to talk about options. She wasn't a great believer, thinking that only "good" options mattered; but just because something is undesirable doesn't mean it's not an option. Sometimes an option has merit, but the timing is wrong. I like these, because I can tuck them away and bring them back when things have changed to make the timing better. In the world of secure payment and identity, there is great potential to do this. Over the past 65 years technology has consistently emerged faster than the market can implement. Sometimes the delay is because of business cases, sometimes it is a matter of partnerships or consortiums that need to be formed and other times consumers simply don't see the need or desire to adopt a new technology. Identifying what needs to be changed and knowing when conditions are right to move ahead has made some people very successful.

Choices are interesting. I've known many people who try hard to make no choices, believing that this is safer than potentially making a wrong choice. The reality is that most choices we make involve other people, so if we don't make the decision, they will. I'd rather be a part of the decision making process than the victim of it. Here is my best advice on making decisions. Get as much information as you deem necessary (avoiding the internet overload scenario) and make sure you include the other people who will be impacted by your decision. Then, if the situation changes or better information becomes available, revisit your decision and change it if necessary. Some people are uncomfortable doing this, afraid that others will view them badly, but what is worse than the decision maker who refuses to embrace a better choice when it becomes available? Make the best decisions you can based on the best information you can get at the time. This too has made many people very successful.

No matter what options are available and what choices you make, there will be outcomes. Take pride in the good ones and share the credit with those who helped you by providing information, supporting your decisions or by challenging you and forcing you to really review every aspect of your choice. If you are going to learn from decisions that didn't work out as well as you had hoped, think about whom else could have helped you. Sometimes you have to accept the fact that your choices were right, but factors beyond your control dictated a bad outcome. And if it simply was your fault, spend the time to figure out what you would do differently the next time.

Choices, options and outcomes are a part of life and a chance to positively succeed.

What do consumers want?

March 2010

Both EMV infrastructure and mobile phones provide opportunities for new payment products and services, but the question is, "what do consumers really want and what are they prepared to pay?"

A word of warning to issuers and research companies - be careful of the questions you ask.

Recent studies show that most Canadians don't see a need for more payment options. Credit, debit and cash meet most of their needs. What they are interested in are products deemed to be more secure. In fact, for the first time in 20 years, we are seeing security surpass convenience as the top consideration related to consumer payment choices. Ubiquity also stays in the top four criteria, along with cost/value.

Your research questions must address all of these if you are going to get an accurate assessment of your opportunity. Lately we have been surveyed more than once about new payment options. One of the surveys was balanced, thorough and clearly the result of a lot of planning by the client and research company. At the end of it, I felt that the questions allowed me to provide objective answers.

The other survey was poorly thought out. By the end of it, I concluded that I had no interest in the product, based on the questions asked. The irony is that I know what that product is really designed for and I can't wait to have it in my wallet!

Security, convenience, ubiquity and cost/value: consumers can't know if they want you're offering until you tell them about all four of these.

Stop - too much information!

May 2011

Last month SAS Canada & Leger marketing reported that 47% of Canadian executives say they are overwhelmed by information. Note - not overloaded, but "overwhelmed". Wikipedia defines overwhelmed as 1. Buried or drowned beneath a huge mass. 2. Defeated completely.

Let's look at the state of our lives and careers. How many of you check your email every morning before you get out of bed? How many of you get more than 100 emails a day or wish you could get it down to a hundred a day? Is it making you better at your job? Does it make your job easier? Does access to limitless information make your employees more productive than 5 years ago?

Information is the new highly addictive junk food and it is fast food delivered via the internet. We need to go on an information diet. For example, I googled "information overload" and it took only 0.18 seconds to return about 4,780,000 results. Even the word "overwhelmed" produced about 32,700,000 results in 0.07 seconds, so when you ask an employee to research a topic, how much is enough?

In the payment sector we are currently looking at social media - Facebook, Twitter, Youtube. We are enthusiastically looking at ways to exploit these new channels, but here are some questions related to that research and information you might want to ask:

1. How much time are your employees spending on research and how much of that work time is bringing benefit to you?
2. How can you increase the value or decrease the time?
3. How do you know that the research is accurate?

I don't have answers to these questions, but I have a baseline when it comes to the use of social media for any of our businesses- it's all about business. It must drive a clear business benefit. If it isn't - it's a problem. The 'C' level question here is "what's in this for us?"

Social media is a new tool. Defining the ROI, processes, procedures, and even developing the controls and determining how to measure success will take a lot of work. Of course you could google it and you would get about 30,400,000 results in 0.19 seconds.

Here is to good questions, good answers and not being overwhelmed by information! Remember - insights outrank information.

Hedging your bets – or betting your career?

October 2013

If you want to launch or change a product or service, there are only three good reasons you can offer your boss or your shareholders. One is to grow your market share, assuming that you won't lose money in the process. The second is that you will make money. The third is that you have to do it to minimize or manage risk.

Spending money to manage risk is just not something that normally leads to great paybacks for employees, unless you can show where it has actually reduced costs. On the other hand, growing market share and profits usually comes with rewards.

So here we are, post EMV. Everyone is anxious to move ahead and there is no shortage of technology to allow us to bet the farm, so to speak. M-commerce, omni-channel, e-wallets, big data and other opportunities are all in the wings. The question is which will drive profit and market share and which won't? Which will help your career and which will hurt it? I don't have the magic ball, but I do know how to get the answers.

Surround yourself with the other stakeholders and learn how this would affect or engage them. Determine how much buyers would pay – or if they would pay. Do the research to determine whether people will become new customers in order to get what you are offering and whether you can keep them if their previous supplier offers it in the future. At the same time, determine whether your customers will leave you if you don't offer it. Don't assume that just because someone else is going to launch something, that there is a need or desire for it.

If you lived through the dot.com era, you'll recognize how easy it is to get caught up in market hype. When a market is projected to be billions you can't help but think that you only need a small piece in order to be successful, but the real success is in filtering the truth from the market noise.

Re-thinking identity management

June 2006

The question of who owns your identity is not as simple to answer as you might think - but it could be if we made a slight shift in how we view the subject.

We bundle many things together when we think of our identity. We may be parents; we certainly are someone's children, we are employees, citizens, consumers and sometimes patients. We bank, shop, travel and do many other things over the course of a day or week.

In that process we often use cards or apps to identify our rights or entitlements to do these transactions. They help identify our related rights and capabilities, but they don't identify us.

Your birth certificate identifies that you were born and the name by which you were identified at birth, or possibly the name you've changed it to. Everything else simply links you to certain transactions such as paying for goods and services; identifies your status such as being Canadian or eligible to drive; or your entitlements such as government paid health care.

In each of these and other cases, a private or public sector entity manages a relationship with you. They enter into agreements with you and provide you with papers, cards or apps for your use. These are all very important to your day-to-day life, but only you own your identity. If you think of it this way, it becomes much easier for third parties to accept that they are a part of your life, but they don't own your identity.

It is much easier to set policies, define rules and establish procedures when that distinction is made.

How do the hard things get done?

October 2008

Your parents knew the answer. Do the right thing. Take it one step at a time. If it is worth doing, it is worth doing right and last but not least, there are no shortcuts to success. Remember?

Every day I hear reasons why things don't get done, but I rarely hear why they can't get done. Why is it that some people can do the hard things and others can't? I think a large part of the answer is because so many people in today's workforce are not held accountable and are not challenged.

When a question is asked, too often the first answer is accepted without any follow up questions. If I'm told that we can't achieve something, shouldn't I ask whether there is something close to it that is achievable? When told that we've tried something in the past and it failed, shouldn't I ask whether conditions have changed since then or if a different approach could work?

Champions get things done. They see questions and challenges as tools, not as reasons to stop progress. As we continue to struggle through hard times we will all need to be champions. We must hold ourselves and others accountable for progress because only those who can get things done will be of value in the workplace. Mom and Dad were right!

Wisdom

Nov / Dec 2008

It occurs to me that wisdom is built on three pillars. The first is the knowledge you gain by learning from others. It starts at birth and never ends. The second is the knowledge you build from experiencing life. This does not come without a price because some of the best lessons learned come from mistakes we have made. The third pillar is character. It determines how you will use the knowledge you've gained from the first two.

Being wise often requires courage and conviction. Wisdom must always be a servant of the long term, not just the immediate future. The wisdom of those who came before us has given us a strong national banking system. Where will our choices take it? How will we add to it? Our health system; what choices must we make to protect it?

Sometimes it is wise to wait before taking action, but it is never wise to wait because you are hoping that a problem will go away and you won't need to think about it.

For 2009, I wish you a prosperous year, one full of wise choices. And as this year passes and you look back, I hope that you've been in a position to make choices that support your long term prosperity.

What did you say?

August 2016

It isn't that we don't speak the same language. The problem isn't in the speaking, or even in the hearing, but in the understanding of both parties. What we say is always interpreted by the listener and that can lead to different types of disconnects.

It could be as simple as speakers and listeners having different definitions of a word. My experience may mean that payment is a credit or debit transaction because that is what I work with, but to my listener it may be a cheque, cash or wire payment.

Another disconnect can be attributed to the fact that every day we have new experiences. When people talk to us, we start to think about what they said and we use our experiences to help us process what we hear. For example, someone comes to you with a new idea, but it isn't new to you. Your experience tells you that it didn't work in the past. Here's the problem. While you were thinking about your own experience the other person kept talking and you didn't hear the thing they said that might have changed your opinion. When you reject their idea, they wonder why you missed their point.

This is not a new phenomenon and it is a large part of why people cite communications as a reason their relationships break down. Whether the relationship is personal or professional, clear communications take work but deliver great results.

I've been in meetings where two people argue vehemently, not understanding that they were actually on the same side. In other meetings I've heard people state their thoughts and watched the body language of the audience reject their ideas. I've also seen that change when someone in the audience starts to ask questions and a dialogue evolves.

Never before has there been a more challenging time in payments, for many reasons. We talk about how quickly technology is being introduced and that is a serious challenge, but how we communicate will make the difference between good or bad business. Who we talk with, the questions we ask, the sharing of our experiences – these are the things that lead to insights.

At ACT Canada we connect people, enable dialogue and drive insights. Let us know if we can help you.

Innovation, education and regulation

December 2003

As we collect the annual nominations for innovation in payments and identity assurance awards, and now that the Payments Review Task Force report has been issued, it is time to reflect on the value of innovation.

If we identify consumers, merchants, issuers and acquirers as the principal stakeholders in payments, innovative payment products and services must balance value and risk for all of them. Technology will always support innovation and we live with the benefits, but as an old friend of mine used to say, "Needs drive the show, not technology".

20 years ago, when I was arguing for the use of smart card technology for payment cards, it would have been innovative, but there was not a compelling need. When fraud became the global need a move to EMV started. Today we have many more opportunities supported by new technology interfaces, devices and applications. Each one has a compelling value proposition for one or more of the prime stakeholder groups, but that may not be enough.

Payments are an essential part of our lives and need to be "protected". The payment card industry has gone to great lengths and considerable expense to mitigate risk. They have required principal stakeholders to do the same by shifting liability to those who fail to employ required security measures.

Canadians have come to expect security in banking and payment based on the accuracy and timeliness of our transactions across the years. We will never know the extent to which regulation contributed to this success, but it did appear to be a positive factor in protecting Canadians from the sub-prime debacle. Continuing on this theme, would consumers be better protected from breaches like the Google wallet if the regulatory playing field was level for all?

We talk about the need to not inhibit innovation, but that can only be within the confines of consumer safety. We regulate food, drugs, electrical appliances and countless other products and services that affect Canadians. We don't allow these sectors to be self-governing.

When it comes to payments, are we inhibiting innovation by holding financial institutions to regulations while allowing others to be self-governing? If we do allow self-governance for one group, what will it take to educate Canadians so they can properly understand the difference between the two and manage their own risks? These are questions that must be asked and answered.

Decisions, opinions, pride and stubbornness

November 2016

We all make decisions based on what we know at the time, but none of us (OK – most of us) don't claim to know everything. When new information becomes available it can validate our earlier decision or cause us to change it.

Many years ago I was in a closed door meeting with federal cabinet ministers. I criticized them for a decision they had made that did not sit well with Canadians. The senior minister present asked me, with more grace than I deserved, what I would have decided had I known specific information that had been available to caucus. He shared that information and I admitted, somewhat sheepishly, that I would have made the same decision they did.

I learned two lessons that day. Never sit in judgement of other people's decisions unless you know what they knew at the time. I also learned that the mature thing to do is to change your mind if new information supports it.

Opinions are just like decisions in this regard. This year we have been bombarded with opinions, many of them political and some of them business. We've seen people who, when provided with new information, have said, "I don't care, I'm not changing my mind". Whether it is caused by pride or stubbornness, taking that position speaks to the person's character. At best it is sad and at worst it is frightening.

One of the great promises that life holds is the possibility of continual learning. It makes life exciting and gives us a sense of hope

Integrity: the hallmark of an individual

August 2009

Throughout your career you meet a lot of people. You will like some but not others. In turn, some will like you and others won't. Wanting to be liked is a normal human reaction, but business gurus always tell us that we need to set that aside in order to succeed.

As I look back, the most memorable people from my career are the ones I respect. I confess that I didn't like all of them, but I admired their integrity. These are the people with whom I'd like to work again.

Integrity doesn't mean you'll always be right but it increases the chances that you and others will be able to accept your mistakes. Standing up for what you believe is right won't always make you popular, but it will make it easier for you to face yourself in the mirror. Defining the line between integrity and stubbornness can be challenging from time to time.

Even more important than the role it plays in building your career, integrity shapes your life. One of the best parts of this job is that I get to work with a number of people whose integrity inspires me. You know who you are and I thank you.

Be inspired by someone you respect and in turn, inspire others.

Has there ever been a more difficult time in payment?

March 2016

Much of the focus on innovation is directed towards millennials, but the 2 most populous groups are millennials and boomers/seniors. In fact, there are more 70 year olds alive today than at any time in history.

Here is the issue. These two groups interface with the world in such different ways that they are forcing us to support significantly diverse ways of doing things. Then it gets even more complex, because physical differences mean that some (read many) seniors can't or won't use the devices that millennials favour. Even service expectations differ. Millennials, they say, don't care if service is friendly as long as it is fast. Seniors expect fast (yes, we are impatient) and friendly service.

Already there is a difference between older and younger, high and low income millennials and you have to think about how they will change as they age. How do you build a strategy for this?

What do we know?

February 2011

Don't you feel that there are more questions surfacing every day?

In the past two weeks I've been travelling and between personal and professional exchanges, I've been surprised by a few things.

One is how often people say "how could we ever do 'X': it's impossible!" Some things look that way, but when you look at the root of a problem or opportunity, it's usually possible to find something similar to learn from. For example: how can we possibly regulate payment or identity security when transactions are web based and international? Do you abide by rules and laws set by the country where the crime was instigated or where the victim was impacted? Seems to be a daunting question, but if we decide that the laws of the victim's country are paramount (or the other way around), then bilateral agreements between countries would come into play, as they already do on many other issues such as trade or border crossing.

Another option is defining global standards, as is the case in major credit cards and many travel documents. It isn't quick, easy or inexpensive, but it is possible and we can get there faster and cheaper by leveraging other solutions already in place. Often we know more than we think we do and can use this knowledge to increase our revenues, reduce our costs or manage risk.

I'm also surprised by how often we think we "know" something because it supports what we want to do. This is often the case when technology makes it possible to enter a new market. For example, while untold billions of dollars have been made because of the emergence of the internet, the dotcom phenomenon ruined countless companies and careers.

Today we have a number of new markets in the incubation phase - mobile commerce being one. We all "think" there is a highly profitable business here, but what we need to "know" is the realistic size of the opportunity and the realistic timeline for getting to the stage of the market where investments can be recouped and profits made. We need to have a clear understanding of the current market and what we need to change in order to pursue that realistic opportunity.

What is leadership?

July 2016

It is a lot easier to talk about what it isn't. Leadership is not just getting to market first. It isn't about building a product or service just because there is a market growth projection that looks like a hockey stick, even though Canadians inherently feel a connection with our national sport. And perhaps, more than anything, leadership isn't about cutting a few pennies per unit to boost the bottom line if it is at the risk of reputational loss or financial penalties. We all agree with this, so why do so many corporate leaders fall into these traps?

I am not trying to justify any of these scenarios, but I will say that it is very hard to know where to invest your resources these days. Part of the problem is social media and the internet. These are breeding grounds for unbridled enthusiasm about every new technology – enthusiasm that rarely leads to self-fulfilling prophecies. Nonetheless, it fosters market buzz and countless organizations then spend money to "take a look".

Research and innovation are both good things and I encourage everyone to invest in them to the extent that makes business sense. It is also good to look back at the past ten years to see how many of your investments had a positive payback. Likely some will and some won't. The key question to ask is which ones, if any, you regret. I can think of some of my own.

Good leaders know what problem they are trying to solve and base their investments on that. Bright shiny objects are only interesting when they solve a problem for someone who is willing to pay for the solution.

In a world awash with information overload, ACT Canada creates clarity by connecting people, enabling dialogue and driving insights. We support good leadership.

Honour!

April 2017

This is one of my last editorials and I'd like to talk about people and careers. Over the past 27 years, I've met some remarkable people. Some were visionaries, some were wizards at executing strategy and a few were both. Some were leaders and some were not.

One of the things they had in common was honour. Each took what they knew and leveraged that with their values and character to make positives changes in the market. It was a pleasure and privilege to have worked with every one of them.

I have also worked with people who were primarily focussed on their own advancement.

People from both groups have enjoyed successful careers, so it is not my place to suggest that you should pursue one path versus the other. However, having said that, I look back at my own career, now that I enter the next stage of my life. I did not set out to run a non-profit stakeholder association but that is what evolved. For the rest of my life, this is the career I'll have to think back on, because there won't be another. That is OK, because I feel good about what ACT Canada has accomplished and my role in that.

Whether you are in the first or second group, the time will come when you'll find yourself thinking back. My wish for you is that you'll feel the same way I do when that time comes.

Honour, decency and integrity. Gifts you give yourself and the world.

Thanks, Mom and Dad

May 2017

I learned a lot from my father, not as much from what he said as from what he did. I learned that "fair" is the best thing to be and that fair allows you to recognize that one side might be better than the other.

I learned the wisdom of knowing the difference between battles and wars and the advantage of choosing which battles to walk away from.

I learned how important it is for people to know your values and that you must be absolutely consistent in adhering to them. If you have to choose between being liked and being respected, I hope you will choose the latter.

I learned that 9 – 5 jobs aren't for everyone. If you are passionate about what you do, those hours won't be enough for you.

I learned that bringing about positive change is hugely rewarding.

From my mother I learned discipline, focus and perseverance, among many other things.

Then there were all the other people who taught me valuable lessons.

What I figured out for myself was that life is full of opportunities to learn and grow and none should be wasted.

Truths – tried and tested

These are a number of things that have been said in the past, but still are relevant today.

It's not about technology

Richard Adamson, President of Coinamatic (retired), makes the case that successful smart card launches are not about technology. They are about building innovative business models that consumers will reward, distribution, scale and convergence that create value for all of the partners in the delivery channel.

Time or money

Every executive will tell you: you can have time or you can have money. With budgets short of money, let's use time to our best advantage.

Technology and privacy

As individuals we constantly assess the risks that we face in the world and make decisions related to minimizing those risks. We must look to technology to protect us, but in doing so we must maintain our ongoing rights to protection of privacy."

Regulation

Privacy is not a technology issue. Technology changes daily, but privacy only shifts as we are threatened. To protect our future privacy rules must be established and must apply across the country. These rules must be clear and adhered to by all those with existing products and services, as well as those bringing new ones into the market. Penalties for failing to follow the rules must be appropriate and be seen to be applied.

Questions

In a world where "we don't know what we don't know", it is the infrequently asked question that can help the most.

Competitors

Most ACT Canada members are competitors of other members, but they face common issues and share common needs.

Go for the gold

Unlike Olympians, you don't get to do your job in front of millions of viewers or stand on the podium when you do it well, but your job is very important. You are important, so go for the gold – every day!

Leaders

Good leaders know what problem they are trying to solve and base their investments on that. Bright shiny objects are only interesting when they solve a problem for someone who is willing to pay for the solution.

Innovation and your career

Today's Payment 2.0 is far more complex than ever before. It is not enough to look at the upside of innovation. Failure to ask questions and hold discussions with all the stakeholder groups may not kill you, but it could kill your career.

Stakeholders and your success

Surround yourself with other stakeholders and learn how they can affect your plans. Involve them in your success.

Payment evolution

Payment is complex and rarely benefits from revolutionary approaches. Evolution allows you to course correct to find the balances between your goals and your customers' expectations.

Strategy

I highly recommend an article called Slow-Motion Automation by Vinnie Mirchandani, published in the Winter 2016 edition of strategy + business. Vinnie looks at technology hype cycles, slow customer adoption curves, incumbents who fight back, tacit knowledge and unintended consequences. Although he is writing about automation, these points are pertinent to all innovation.

Walls and technology

It is important to know what a technology can do and to be enthusiastic about its potential. It is equally important to know how and when the market will react / adopt. After all, when you know there's a wall, you can bring a ladder!

Boy – did they get it wrong!

Not everyone has a good crystal ball. Here are some of the "oops, did I say that" quotes.

In the 30's - "Who the hell wants to hear actors talk?" Jack Warner
In the 60's - "we only see a market for a dozen large computers" President of IBM
1971 - "People won't pay for cable T.V."
1976 - "Computers are only for big business and corporations."
1977 - "Who will ever use a fax machine?"
1983 - "I don't want / need a cell phone."
1989 - "CD's will never replace diskettes."

And my personal favourite "boy did they get it wrong"...

"10K, why would I ever need a computer with 10K of memory" Catherine Johnston, 1980

Appendix A - Market Review

2016 Key highlights...

- ACT Canada continued to bring stakeholder groups together to discuss areas of concern and opportunities. At Cardware, retailers and financial institutions came together to discuss:
  - their joint customer's experiences
  - concerns about the potential of 8 digit bins
  - the future of biometric authentication for e-commerce and at the point-of-sale
  - contactless certification implications for merchants
  - Payment Account Reference (PAR) potentially used with tokenization when the PAN is no longer available
  - liability shift for tap (contactless)
  - authentication for online processing
  - a preferred single integration for loyalty
  - the potential for a consortium to determine a centralized method to share information between merchants and issuers.
- ACT Canada negotiates free listings for members in the GSMA online marketplace with discounts on any upgraded listings, and discounts for 14 external conferences

Metrics
- 27 member events / workgroups
- 15 publications / reports / papers
- 11 speeches / briefings
- 3 government interactions
- 45 speakers at Cardware

The market...

- The 2 most populous groups are millennials and boomers/seniors. In fact, there are more 70 year olds alive than at any time in history. In spite of this, millennials are the focus of the financial sector.
- Fintech, blockchain applications, faster payment and biometric authentication dominated market discussions over the year with aggregated loyalty, digital currency, IoT payments, mPOS and iPOS, real time payment, P2P, and mobile wallets also being of interest to many stakeholders

Board of Directors

Christian Ali	Dream Payment
Jeremy Bornstein	MasterCard
David Chaudhari	Ingenico Canada, Ltd.
Pawel Chrobok	Visa Canada
Derek Colfer	Visa Canada
Jeff Ecker	TDMS
John Flett	CanCard Inc
Owen Gingras	Walmart Canada Corp.
Doug Hatton	Moneris
Robert Hayhow	Equinox
Brian Hirman	Gemalto
Caroline Hubberstey	Interac Association
Catherine Johnston	ACT Canada
Doug Macdonald	MNP
Jonathan Magder	Accenture
Carol Maietta	Central 1 Credit Union
Wendy Maisey	ICC Solutions
Todd Roberts	CIBC
Paul Zatychec	EWA-Canada Ltd.

ACT Canada notes of interest

Andrea McMullen is promoted to the position of President and Catherine Johnston retains the position of CEO

2016

Bringing members together and building an informed market

ACT Canada Member Events, Teams and Workgroups	Publications, Reports, Papers & Media	Speeches
<ul><li>ACTive Networking (x2)</li><li>Annual General Meeting</li><li>Biometrics for payments - merchants and acquirers workshop (Niagara Falls)</li><li>Board Advisory Committee</li><li>Cardware 2016: Strategic Innovation (Niagara Falls)</li><li>Cardware Connections (Toronto) - Biometric Authentication</li><li>Cardware Connections (Toronto) – Biometric Authentication – Stakeholder Questions</li><li>Cardware Connections closed door briefings - Vancouver, Edmonton, Ottawa, Montreal - Payments 2016: What's causing CEOs to lose sleep and how does that affect you</li><li>FinTech Pitches</li><li>Issuers and Merchants breakfast</li><li>Issues Alert team</li><li>IVIE Awards</li><li>Merchant Strategic Leadership team</li><li>Merchants and Payment Networks closed door meetings</li><li>Mobile Strategic Leadership team</li><li>Payments Bootcamp (Toronto, Vancouver, Edmonton, Niagara Falls)</li><li>President's Advisory Council</li><li>Quantum Computing and Financial Services</li><li>SLTs amalgamate to form the Payment Stakeholders SLT</li><li>Women in Payments networking and charity fundraiser</li></ul>	<ul><li>ACT news - driving insights (11 editions)</li><li>Are Conferences a Waste of Time?</li><li>FINTECH: a different perspective -Media Planet</li><li>Members Directory</li><li>Will that be cash or contactless?</li></ul>	<ul><li>ATMIA Canada conference - moderator</li><li>Cambridge Security Forum – participant</li><li>Canadian Update ETA Transact 16 (Las Vegas) -</li><li>How is Canada tackling payment? Transact 16 (ETA) Strategic Innovation</li><li>Merchant Advisory Group (MAG) – Fostering Merchant and Financial Institution Collaboration in Payment: SIG Facilitator</li><li>Mobile Payments Conference – Payments panel moderator</li><li>Payment Innovation from possible to inevitable: what needs to change Cardware 2016 — panel moderator</li><li>What's Causing CEOs to Lose Sleep and How Does That Affect You? Cardware Connections – (4)</li></ul>

ACT Canada Member Events, Teams and Workgroups	External Events (other)	Government Key Interactions
Continued from previous page ▫ In-house training for a western FI ▫ Members receive free listings in the GSMA online marketplace and discounts on any upgraded listings, negotiated by ACT Canada ▫ Members received discounts for 14 external conferences, negotiated by ACT Canada	▫ All Payments Expo (New Orleans) ▫ Connect ID (Washington) ▫ Mobile World Congress (Barcelona) ▫ Money 20/20 (Copenhagen & Las Vegas) ▫ MRC Conference (Las Vegas) ▫ Payments Summit (Orlando) ▫ Trustech (Cannes)	▫ FCAC, FinPay & CPA meetings (Ottawa)

and in the...

- 800,000 CUSTOMERS NOW USING COMPASS CARD: TRANSLINK CEO.
- ACCEO AND TRURATING PARTNER TO SIMPLIFY MERCHANTS' AND RETAILERS' INSTANT VISIBILITY ON KEY CUSTOMER EXPERIENCE METRICS.
- ACCEO TENDER RETAIL PARTNERS WITH SYSTEM INNOVATORS.
- AIR CANADA AND CIBC LAUNCH MULTICURRENCY PREPAID CARD FOR TRAVELLERS.
- AMERICAN EXPRESS CHANGES THE FACE OF REWARDS IN CANADA ALLOWING CARDMEMBERS TO USE POINTS FOR ANY PURCHASE USING THE AMEX APP.
- APPLE PAY EXPANDS IN CANADA WITH SUPPORT FROM MAJOR BANKS FOR DEBIT AND CREDIT CARDS.
- APPLE PAY NOW AVAILABLE TO DESJARDINS MEMBERS AND CUSTOMERS.
- BMO, MASTERCARD ROLL OUT BIOMETRIC CORPORATE CARD PROGRAM.
- CANADA'S CREDIT UNIONS OFFER MOBILE PAY SERVICE WITH MOBILE INTERAC FLASH - THE NEW SOLUTION LEVERAGES THE INTERAC TOKEN SERVICE PROVIDER.
- CANADA'S CREDIT UNIONS WIN BIG FOR MOBILE PAY.
- CANADA'S FINTECH ECOSYSTEM IS GAINING MOMENTUM AS A GLOBAL HUB FOR INNOVATIVE TECHNOLOGY.
- CANADIAN NFC MOBILE WALLET SURETAP TO CLOSE DOWN.
- CANADIAN OPEN-LOOP PREPAID MARKET HITS $3.1 BILLION IN 2015.
- CANADIAN PAYMENT METHODS AND TRENDS REPORT FINDS CASH IS KING, FOR NOW.
- CANADIAN PAYMENTS MARKET TRANSITION: A STUDY BY THE CANADIAN PAYMENTS ASSOCIATION.
- CANADIAN VENDING GROUP SET TO ADD MOBILE PAYMENTS TO MACHINES NATIONWIDE.
- CARDTEK AND NXP COLLABORATE TO

- INTRODUCE DIGITAL PAYMENT SOLUTION FOR WEARABLES
- CARDTEK, DC PAYMENTS TO LAUNCH MOBILE PAYMENT SOLUTION IN CANADA.
- CENTRAL 1 ACCELERATES OMNI-CHANNEL SERVICES STRATEGY IN COLLABORATION WITH CGI.
- CENTRAL 1 LAUNCHES FIRST FULLY INTEGRATED OPEN ANYWHERE ONLINE AND MOBILE ACCOUNT OPENING WITH CONEXUS CREDIT UNION.
- CIBC FORMS STRATEGIC ALLIANCE WITH NATIONAL AUSTRALIA BANK AND ISRAEL'S BANK LEUMI.
- CIBC PARTNERS WITH MAGNUSCARDS ON A BANKING APP THAT HELPS PEOPLE WITH SPECIAL NEEDS.
- CPA LEADS TRANSITION TO ELECTRONIC PAYMENTS WITH LAUNCH OF GLOBAL MESSAGING STANDARD IN CANADA.
- CPA SEEKS FEEDBACK ON ENHANCEMENTS TO POINT-OF-SERVICE PAYMENTS FRAMEWORK & ANNOUNCES NAME CHANGE.
- CPI CARD GROUP-CANADA INC. SELECTED BY ONTARIO LOTTERY AND GAMING CORPORATION AS MANUFACTURER FOR FIRST-EVER CANADIAN LOTTERY GIFT CARD PROGRAM.
- DESJARDINS AND MASTERCARD BRING NEW PAYMENT OPTIONS TO CANADIANS.
- DIRECTCASH BANK NOW OFFERING BULK INTERAC E-TRANSFER SERVICE TO BUSINESS CLIENTS.
- DREAM PAYMENTS LAUNCHES MOBILE MERCHANT SERVICES PLATFORM FOR BANKS AND MERCHANT ACQUIRERS.
- ELAVON DELIVERS APPLE PAY FOR CANADIAN BUSINESSES.
- ELAVON LAUNCHES NEW TABLET-BASED PAYMENT PRODUCT IN CANADA.
- EQUINOX AND ACCEO PARTNER TO DELIVER INTEGRATED RETAIL PAYMENT SOLUTION.
- ETHOCA WINS 2016 ACT CANADA IVIE AWARD FOR CANADIAN INNOVATION BENEFITTING MERCHANTS.

Canadian news

- FLEXITI FINANCIAL (FORMERLY WELLSPRING FINANCIAL) AND LIQUID CAPITAL ANNOUNCE CREDIT FACILITY TO SUPPORT GROWTH OF ITS CONSUMER FINANCE BUSINESS IN CANADA.
- HAVE IDEAS ON HELPING CANADIANS MANAGE DEBT? CALLING ALL INNOVATORS TO SCOTIABANK'S FIRST HACKATHON.
- HOME TRUST AND GIANT TIGER LAUNCH NEW GIANT TIGER REWARDS VISA CARD.
- ICC SOLUTIONS WINS TWO ACT CANADA INTERNATIONAL INNOVATION AWARDS.
- INGENICO GROUP AND NANOPAY CORPORATION PARTNER TO ENABLE CANADIAN RETAILERS TO ACCEPT MINTCHIP DIGITAL CASH.
- INGENICO GROUP NAMES SUZAN DENONCOURT MANAGING DIRECTOR FOR CANADA.
- INTERAC COLLABORATES WITH NORWAY'S BANKAXEPT.
- INTERAC DEBIT CARD FRAUD LOSSES PLUMMET FOR THE SIXTH CONSECUTIVE YEAR.
- INTERAC NAMED MOST INNOVATIVE ORGANIZATION BY ACT CANADA.
- INTERAC PAYMENT INNOVATION ACCELERATING GROWTH OF DIGITAL PAYMENTS IN CANADA.
- MASTERCARD AND BMO MAKE FINGERPRINT AND 'SELFIE' PAYMENT TECHNOLOGY A REALITY IN NORTH AMERICA.
- MNP EXPANDS CYBERSECURITY SERVICES BY MERGING IN NCI, A LEADING CYBERSECURITY FIRM.
- MOBEEWAVE EXPANDS P2P APP ACROSS CANADA.
- MOBILE PAYMENT USE CONTINUES TO INCREASE IN CANADA.
- MOBILE PAYMENTS COME TO CANADIAN CREDIT UNIONS.
- MONERIS DELIVERS NEW TOOLS AND RESOURCES FOR DEVELOPERS.
- MONERIS LAUNCHES BUSINESS-TO-BUSINESS PAYMENT SOLUTIONS TO OPTIMIZE COMMERCIAL CARD ACCEPTANCE.
- MONERIS THE FIRST NORTH AMERICAN PROCESSOR TO BE ABLE TO SELF-CERTIFY EMV SOLUTIONS FOR FIVE MAJOR CARD BRANDS.
- NANOPAY ACQUIRES MINTCHIP FROM THE ROYAL CANADIAN MINT.
- NANOPAY ANNOUNCES THE DEPLOYMENT OF MINTCHIP DIGITAL CURRENCY.
- NEW APP LETS CANADIANS APPLY FOR A MORTGAGE WITH A TAP OF THEIR SMARTPHONE.
- NEW CREDIT UNION ASSOCIATION LAUNCHES IN CANADA: CANADIAN CREDIT UNION ASSOCIATION.
- OT STRENGTHENS ITS PORTFOLIO IN CANADA WITH INTERAC-CERTIFIED DUAL-INTERFACE CARD AND ONLINE FRAUD REDUCTION TECHNOLOGY.
- PIVOTAL PAYMENTS BECOMES INTERAC ASSOCIATION DIRECT CONNECTOR, STRENGTHENING ITS CANADIAN PAYMENTS INFRASTRUCTURE.
- RBC INVESTS IN MACHINE LEARNING THROUGH PARTNERSHIP WITH THE UNIVERSITY OF TORONTO.
- SAMSUNG CANADA PARTNERS WITH CIBC TO BRING MOBILE PAYMENTS TO CANADIANS.
- SCOTIABANK LAUNCHES APPLE PAY FOR DEBIT AND CREDIT CARD CUSTOMERS IN CANADA.
- SENSIBILL BRINGS DIGITAL RECEIPTS TO CANADA WITH UGO PARTNERSHIP.
- STARBUCKS EXPANDS MOBILE ORDERING SERVICES IN TORONTO, VANCOUVER.
- SURETAP ADDS LOYALTY TO BECOME CANADA'S MOST REWARDING DIGITAL WALLET.
- SURETAP AND ENSTREAM TAKE BIG STEPS FORWARD WITH SOCIETÉ DE TRANSPORT DE MONTREAL IN MOBILE TICKETING.
- TANGERINE FIRST BANK IN CANADA TO LAUNCH 'EYEVERIFY', 'VOCALPASSWORD' AND IN-APP SECURE CHAT.
- TD ADOPTS VISA'S SECURE TOKENIZATION TECHNOLOGY, ENHANCING CUSTOMERS' MOBILE PAYMENT EXPERIENCE.
- TD STRENGTHENS LEADERSHIP IN DIGITAL WITH THE LAUNCH OF APPLE PAY; DELIVERING MORE CHOICE TO MORE CANADIANS THAN ANY OTHER BANK.
- TORONTO'S DREAM PAYMENTS WINS GLOBAL FINTECH CHALLENGE.
- TSYS CANADIAN STUDY HIGHLIGHTS RESILIENCY OF CREDIT, DEBIT AND CASH.

- VERIFONE EXPANDS SERVICES OFFERING FOR LARGE RETAILERS IN THE US AND CANADA WITH AGREEMENT TO ACQUIRE AJB SOFTWARE.
- VISA AND INGENICO COMBINE CONTACTLESS PAYMENTS WITH DIGITAL SIGNAGE AT TIFF.
- WALMART CANADA LAUNCHES SHOPPING APP AS MOBILE BECOMES BIGGEST TRAFFIC-DRIVER.
- WHAT SAMSUNG PAY MEANS FOR CANADIANS.
- WHAT'S IN THE CARDS FOR US AND CANADA PAYMENTS (LITERALLY)?
- WHY CANADA IS BLOCKCHAIN'S BIGGEST HOT SPOT.

2015 Key highlights...

■ Through 4 member-initiated Strategic Leadership teams and other services, ACT Canada helped members focus on:

- cross border mag stripe fraud
- ESD damage to cards and terminals
- the impact of Contactless Certification on all stakeholder groups
- uncertainty as to where to invest
- tokenization, encryption and customer authentication
- steady but slow EMV progress in the US
- market reaction to Apple Pay, SamsungPay and other digital wallets
- issues resulting from lack of cross stakeholder dialogue
- the move to immediate "or faster" payment
- the need to upgrade FI infrastructure in Canada
- the role of fin-tech
- market issues and opportunities

Metrics

- 23 member events / workgroups
- 30 publications/reports/papers
- 7 speeches / briefings
- 2 government consultation

The market...

- 2015 was a challenging year for our members, as well as for the association.
- For members, it was about deciding where to support innovation, with the EMV rollout substantially finished in Canada.
- The Interac mandate for EMV compliant POS comes into effect
- Apple Pay launches in Canada
- Canada moves to modernize our payments infrastructure
- Canadian Parliament report recommends a 'light touch' in virtual-currency regulation
- Trends, security, collaboration and innovation are focal points

ACT Canada notes of interest

- ACT advocates that ISO review and amend ESD tolerance standard

- My favourite comment from Cardware was the answer to "what problem is being solved by digital currency?" The answer was "if it is p2p payments we should find a way to improve our current solutions. Digital currency is an expensive and complicated way to solve p2p."

- ACTive Networking is introduced to provide an informal complement to Cardware Connections

2015

Bringing members together and building an informed market

ACT Canada Member Events, Teams & Workgroups	Publications, Reports, Papers & Media	Speeches, Briefings
<ul><li>ACTive networking launched</li><li>Annual General Meeting</li><li>Board Advisory Committee</li><li>Cardware 2015: Payment and Digital ID Insights</li><li>Cardware Connections Networking – Innovation Strategy</li><li>Cardware Connections Networking event - Before You invest: 50 questions that need to be asked and answered</li><li>Customer Authentication Strategic Leadership team (report at Cardware)</li><li>Issues Alert team</li><li>IVIEs Innovation Awards Gala</li><li>Member closed door briefings - Vancouver, Calgary, Ottawa, Montreal</li><li>Merchant Data Breach Avoidance meeting</li><li>Merchant Mobile Strategy Meeting</li><li>Merchant Strategic Leadership team</li><li>Merchants and Payment Networks closed door meetings</li><li>Mobile Payments Seminar (with Payments Business Magazine)</li><li>Mobile Strategic Leadership team (report at Cardware)</li><li>Multi-app Issuance Strategic Leadership team</li><li>Payment Acceptance Strategic Leadership team (formerly POS)</li><li>Prepaid Cards Strategic Leadership team</li><li>President's Advisory Council</li></ul>	<ul><li>*16 x 9* interview</li><li>*A national cybersecurity solution proposal for Canada's retail industry*</li><li>ACT news - driving insights (11 editions)</li><li>*Allow me to rant for a minute*</li><li>*Best EMV Practices*</li><li>*Best EMV practices for merchants*</li><li>*Cards, Cards, Cards* - Payments Business magazine interview</li><li>*Cashless Payment in Canada* Canadian Vending Magazine – interview</li><li>*Contactless Certification* report is completed and contains recommendations for changes</li><li>*Cyber Security and Compliance*</li><li>*Data: big and small*</li><li>*ESD report* is completed and recommendations are made to ISO</li><li>*M-Commerce: What Does the Consumer Want?*</li><li>*Members Directory*</li><li>*Mitigating online payment risk*</li><li>*Online Fraud* Global TV</li><li>*Payment Innovation: Questions that must be asked and answered before you invest*</li><li>Payments Business Magazine (4 articles)</li><li>*Secure ID Report: Meeting the Needs of Governments and Citizens*</li><li>*Wearables: new or improved?*</li><li>*What does the Consumer Want?*</li></ul>	<ul><li>*Are we ready for chip and PIN?* MAG</li><li>*Canada Report* 3rd World IC Conference (China) -</li><li>*EMV and Beyond: Lessons Learned from Across the Pond* ETA's Transact 15 (San Francisco) -</li><li>*EMV track Chair & EMV: the best way to reduce fraud -* panel moderator Cartes North America (Washington)</li><li>*Innovation in Payment Systems and Finance* Canadian Financing and Leasing Association (Gatineau) (workshop) – panel moderator</li><li>*Is There a Real Future for NFC and Contactless?* MAG (San Antonio) - Back to the Future</li><li>*Technology is easy – everything else is hard! Workshop* Global e-ID Conference 2015 (Washington) -</li></ul>

Key Additional Member Services	External Events (other)	Government Key Consultations
<ul><li>14 international conferences give ACT Canada members discounts</li><li>1 member education day</li><li>Members use discounts at Cardware</li></ul>	<ul><li>Mobile World Congress (Barcelona)</li><li>Money 20/20 (Las Vegas)</li><li>Smart Card Alliance Payments Summit 2015 (Salt Lake City)</li></ul>	<ul><li>Department of Finance Canada, responded to the request for consultation on "Balancing Oversight and Innovation in the Ways We Pay"</li><li>Federal Privacy Commissioner's office invites us to review their Payment Document pre-publication</li></ul>

and in the...

- ACCENTURE SURVEYED 4,000 CONSUMERS IN NORTH AMERICA TO UNDERSTAND THEIR ATTITUDES ABOUT PAYMENTS AND HOW THEY ANTICIPATE MAKING PAYMENTS BY 2020.

- ACCEO SOLUTIONS ACQUIRES TORONTO FIRM MULTIPOST

- ACT CANADA CONGRATULATES THE WINNERS OF THE IVIE AWARDS

- AIR MILES GIVES CANADIANS A NEW WAY TO PAY IT FORWARD

- AMERICAN EXPRESS CANADA TAKES ANOTHER STEP FORWARD IN DIGITAL INNOVATION

- APPLE PAY EXPANDING TO CANADA WITHOUT CANADIAN BANKS

- APPLE PAY LAUNCHES IN CANADA WITHOUT COOPERATION FROM CANADIAN BANKS

- APPLE PAY'S EXPANSION TO CANADA FACES COST AND SECURITY QUESTIONS

- APPLE PAY'S CANADIAN PLANS

- AT THE SPEED OF SOUND: RBC CONVERSATIONAL VOICE BIOMETRICS A CANADIAN FIRST

- BECK TAXI LAUNCHES MOBILE APP WITH PAYPAL AND CREDIT CARD IN-APP PAYMENT

- BEST BUY CANADA CHOOSES DESJARDINS TO MANAGE ITS PRIVATE LABEL CREDIT CARD PORTFOLIO

- BMO HARRIS BANK UNVEILS CARDLESS APP

- CALGARY LOOKS AT LAUNCHING SMARTPHONE TICKETING SYSTEM

- CAN APPLE PAY MAKE ITS FINANCIAL MARK IN CANADA?

- CANADA MOVES TO MODERNIZE PAYMENTS INFRASTRUCTURE

- CANADIAN COFFEE CHAIN GOES MOBILE WITH LOYALTY PLATFORM

- CANADIAN GIFT TRENDS SURVEY FINDS GIFT CARDS ARE THE MOST POPULAR GIFT THIS HOLIDAY SEASON

Canadian news

- CANADIAN GOVERNMENT EXTENDS CODE OF CONDUCT TO MOBILE PAYMENTS

- CANADIAN NEWS

- CANADIAN PARLIAMENT REPORT RECOMMENDS A 'LIGHT TOUCH' IN VIRTUAL-CURRENCY REGULATION

- CANADIAN TIRE ADDS DIGITAL NOTES TO ITS BRICKS-AND-MORTAR PLAYLIST

- CANADIAN TIRE ENTERS MOBILE WALLET MARKET WITH MPAY & PLAY

- CANADIANS PAY CASH LESS THAN HALF THE TIME, BANK OF CANADA CALCULATES

- CANADIANS PRIORITIZE SECURITY OVER CONVENIENCE, SPEED WHEN MAKING PAYMENTS

- CANADIANS THROWING AWAY MONEY IN UNUSED GIFT CARDS

- CFIB, CHASE PAYMENTECH DELIVER CREDIT CARD SAVINGS FOR SMALL BUSINESS

- CIBC ANNOUNCES PARTNERSHIP WITH MARS DISCOVERY DISTRICT TO DRIVE INNOVATION

- CIBC FIRST CANADIAN BANK TO PARTICIPATE IN SURETAP(TM) OPEN MOBILE WALLET

- CIBC FIRST CANADIAN BANK TO SUPPORT CLIENT ENROLMENT ON VISA CHECKOUT

- COLLABRIA ANNOUNCES NEW PARTNERSHIP WITH KAWARTHA CREDIT UNION

- CREATING NEW OPPORTUNITIES IN CANADIAN PAYMENTS: CPA SEEKING FEEDBACK ON ITS ISO 20022 PAYMENTS STANDARD INITIATIVE

- DESJARDINS GROUP ESTABLISHES AGREEMENT TO JOIN SECUREKEY CONCIERGE AUTHENTICATION SERVICE

- DESJARDINS LAUNCHES TWO NEW MOBILE PAYMENT SOLUTIONS FOR SMALL BUSINESSES AND SELF-EMPLOYED WORKERS

- DIRECTCASH PAYMENTS INC. ANNOUNCES LAUNCH OF DC TAG

- DREAM PAYMENTS LAUNCHES CANADA'S FIRST OFF-THE-SHELF EMV PAYMENT TERMINAL THAT ACCEPTS INTERAC DEBIT CARD PAYMENTS
- EUROPE 'WINNING THE WAR' ON CNP FRAUD
- EVERLINK INTRODUCES INTERAC FLASH ENABLED WEARABLE PAYMENTS SOLUTION
- FBI: RANSOMWARE NETS CRIMINALS $18 MILLION IN BITCOIN
- FIRST REACTION TO APPLE PAY IN CANADA IS NOT A GOOD SIGN FOR VISA AND MASTERCARD
- GLOBAL PAYMENTS & DISCOVER FINANCIAL SERVICES ANNOUNCE STREAMLINED CARD ACCEPTANCE ON THE DISCOVER GLOBAL NETWORK IN CANADA
- GLOBAL PAYMENTS ANNOUNCES FULL-SERVICE ACQUIRING FOR AMERICAN EXPRESS SMALL BUSINESS MERCHANTS WITH THE ROLL-OUT OF OPTBLUE IN CANADA
- GLOBAL PAYMENTS LAUNCHES EMV & CONTACTLESS MOBILE PAYMENTS SOLUTION IN CANADA
- GLOBAL PAYMENTS LAUNCHES EMV AND CONTACTLESS MOBILE PAYMENTS SOLUTION IN CANADA
- GLOBAL PAYMENTS WORKS WITH MERCHANTS IN CANADA ON MOBILE PAYMENTS, LOYALTY
- HOME TRUST COMPANY TO ACQUIRE CFF BANK
- INCREASING SECURITY OF MOBILE PAYMENTS FOR CANADIANS WITH RBC WALLET
- INGENICO, GOOGLE PARTNER ON CROSS-BORDER E-COMMERCE PILOT
- INTERAC DEBIT CARD FRAUD LOSSES FALL TO RECORD LOW
- IOT? "NEVER HEARD OF IT," SAY OVER HALF OF CANADIAN BUSINESSES
- MANULIFE BANK TO ADD MORE THAN 800 AUTOMATED BANKING MACHINES ACROSS CANADA
- MARS PARTNERS WITH PAYPAL, UGO AND MONERIS SOLUTIONS TO POWER FINANCIAL TECHNOLOGY INNOVATION IN CANADA
- MOBILE TICKETING COMES TO TORONTO'S TRANSIT SYSTEM
- MONERIS DRIVES BUSINESSES TO MOBILE SOLUTIONS
- MONERIS INTRODUCES 'VERIFY' TO HELP FIGHT $1.7B IN CANADIAN RETAIL FRAUD
- MONERIS MAKES CHECKOUT EASY FOR RETAILERS AND CONSUMERS WITH PAYD PRO PLUS
- MONERIS MAKES EMV MPOS LINE AVAILABLE IN US
- MONERIS SELECTED AS PAYMENT ACQUIRER FOR GOVERNMENT OF CANADA
- MONERIS TO OFFER MERCHANTS NEXT-GENERATION POWA TECHNOLOGIES SALES AND MARKETING SOLUTION
- MONERIS WORKS WITH VERIFONE TO OFFER ONE OF THE FIRST EMV-CERTIFIED UNATTENDED PAYMENT SOLUTIONS IN THE UNITED STATES
- NORDSTROM AND TD BANK GROUP ANNOUNCE STRATEGIC CREDIT CARD RELATIONSHIP
- NORTH AMERICAN CONSUMERS OVERWHELMINGLY TRUST BANKS TO SECURELY MANAGE THEIR PERSONAL DATA, ACCORDING TO ACCENTURE REPORT
- NOW IS THE TIME FOR BANKS TO DETERMINE MOBILE PAY STRATEGY
- PAYPAL BRINGS 'ONE TOUCH' PAYMENTS TO CANADA FOR FASTER CHECKOUTS
- PAYPAL TIES UP WITH BLACKBERRY TO PROVIDE PEER-TO-PEER (P2P) PAYMENTS THROUGH BBM CHATS
- RBC FIRST BANK IN NORTH AMERICA WITH HOST CARD EMULATION
- RBC IS TESTING APPLE PAY, RUMORED TO BE LAUNCHING IN CANADA SOON
- RBC WILL WORK TOWARDS STRENGTHENING MOBILE PAYMENTS SECURITY WITH ITS NEW PATENT
- REPORT: CROSS-BORDER B2C E-COMMERCE TO HIT $1 TRILLION IN 2020
- ROGERS BRINGS ITS SURETAP WALLET SERVICE TO TELUS AND BELL DEVICES
- ROGERS PAYMENT SOLUTION SURETAP SPUN OFF, TO LAUNCH NEW MOBILE WALLET PRODUCT

- SASKTEL & MTS TEAM UP TO EXPAND MOBILE PAYMENTS IN CANADA
- SASKTEL TO LAUNCH PAY WITH YOUR PHONE CAPABILITY
- SCOTIABANK EXPANDS MOBILE PAYMENT SERVICE
- SCOTIABANK FIRST CANADIAN BANK TO LAUNCH BULK INTERAC E-TRANSFER SERVICE
- SOBEYS, SOBEYS URBAN FRESH AND FOODLAND STORES TO LAUNCH AIR MILES REWARD PROGRAM ACROSS ONTARIO
- SQUARE BUYS TORONTO'S KILI TECHNOLOGY
- STARBUCKS' MOBILE ORDER & PAY POISED TO EXPAND TO UK, CANADA & 21 MORE US STATES
- STARBUCKS RELEASE OF MOBILE ORDER & PAY IN CANADA IS ABOUT DATA
- SURETAP EXPANDS PAYMENT OPTIONS WITH INTRODUCTION OF VIRTUAL RELOADABLE PREPAID CARD
- SURETAP PARTNERS WITH POINTS, BECOMES FIRST CANADIAN MOBILE WALLET TO OFFER FULL LOYALTY INTEGRATION
- TD BANK PARTNERS WITH TORONTO STARTUP TO BRING MORE PERSONALIZATION TO ITS BANKING APP
- TELUS AND CIBC TEAM UP TO ADD VALUE TO CANADIANS' EVERYDAY PURCHASES WITH NEW CREDIT CARD
- TEXT US: TD THE FIRST MAJOR BANK IN CANADA TO OFFER SMS CUSTOMER SERVICE
- THE NORTH WEST COMPANY INTRODUCES FIRST SCALABLE DIRECT DEPOSIT SOLUTION FOR PREPAID CARDS TO STORES ACROSS NORTHERN CANADA
- TORONTO SUBWAY GETS CARD PAYMENT OPTION
- TSYS RELEASES '2014 CANADIAN CONSUMER PAYMENT CHOICE STUDY'
- TSYS RESEARCH REVEALS CANADIAN CONSUMERS PREFER CREDIT CARDS AS PAYMENT CHOICE
- TSYS SIGNS PAYMENTS AGREEMENT WITH TANGERINE BANK
- TTC TO FULLY SWITCH TO PRESTO CARDS; WILL STOP ACCEPTING TICKETS, TOKENS IN 2017
- UGO WALLET EXPANDS CAPABILITIES TO INCLUDE MORE LOYALTY CARDS
- UNIONPAY HITS 5 BILLION ISSUED MARK
- VISA INC. AND VERIFONE JOIN FORCES TO ACCELERATE OMNI COMMERCE GLOBALLY
- WENDY MAISEY NAMED AS THE RECIPIENT OF ACT CANADA'S 2015 HERO'S AWARD
- WHITE PAPER OUTLINES PRINCIPLES FOR SECURE, WIDE-SCALE ADOPTION OF INNOVATIVE PRODUCTS AND SERVICES IN THE CANADIAN PAYMENT INDUSTRY

2014 Key highlights...

- Through 4 member initiated Strategic Leadership teams and other services, ACT Canada helped members focus on:
  - payment, m-commerce and digital identity
  - market issues and opportunities

and find answers to:
  - "Where is the money in mobile?"
  - "When will cross border counterfeit losses stop?"
  - "How Do We Raise the Bar on Secure ID?"
  - "What is the right Customer Authentication to deal with Card-Not-Present fraud?"
  - "Is it time for a multi-application card?"
  - "How much innovation is affordable?"
  - "How do I find the right people to hire?"
  - and many more questions

Metrics

  - 16 member events / workgroups
  - 29 publications / reports / papers
  - 13 speeches / briefings
  - 7 government consultations

The market...

  - Fear of missing out continues to compete with ROI
  - There is new optimism with Apple's adoption of NFC
  - New stakeholder groups are involved in payment, m-commerce and digital identity
  - Stakeholders struggle with the impacts of ESD and non-harmonized contactless certification
  - Because there are many new stakeholder groups involved in payment, m-commerce and digital identity, there is an increased risk of unintended consequences when they are not all involved in the planning processes

Board of Directors

Christian Ali	SecureKey Technologies Inc.
Tracey Black	GFH Group
David Chaudhari	Ingenico Canada, Ltd.
Pawel Chrobok	EnStream LP
Jason Davies	MasterCard
Owen Gingras	Walmart Canada Corp.
Lorna Johnson	Interac Association/Acxsys Corporation
Catherine Johnston	ACT Canada
Karrie MacDonald	Gemalto
Dave Metcalfe	Scotiabank
Wendy Maisey	ICC Solutions Ltd
Didier Serra	SecureKey Technologies
Paul Zatychec	EWA-Canada Ltd.

ACT Canada notes of interest

- ACT hits 25 year milestone
- Members ask for our help with EMV interoperability issues north of the border and our help in promoting a timely rollout of EMV south of the border
- Introduction of Start-up membership class
- 1551 individuals are represented within our corporate members
- 130+ members participate in strategic leadership teams at 40+ meetings

2014

Bringing members together and building an informed market

ACT Canada Member Events, Teams & Workgroups	Publications, Reports, Papers & Media	Speeches
<ul><li>3rd Annual Women in Payments Networking meet, greet and charity event</li><li>Annual General Meeting</li><li>Board Advisory Committee</li><li>Cardware 2014: Payment and Digital ID Insights Niagara Falls</li><li>Cardware Connections member networking event</li><li>Customer Authentication Strategic Leadership team</li><li>Innovation Awards Gala</li><li>Innovation Showcase launched at Cardware</li><li>Issues Alert / Management team</li><li>M-Commerce (Mobile) Strategic Leadership team</li><li>Merchant and Payment Networks closed door meetings</li><li>Mobile Payment Training workshop (Payments Business Magazine - partner)</li><li>Mobile Strategic Leadership team</li><li>Multi-app Issuance Strategic Leadership team</li><li>Payment Acceptance team (formerly the POS team) - ongoing work on contactless certification issue and ESD</li><li>President's Advisory Council</li></ul>	<ul><li>ACT news - driving insights (11 editions)</li><li>*Best EMV practices for merchants*</li><li>*Bitcoin and Canadians*</li><li>*Card Evolution*</li><li>*Contactless Certification Stakeholder Impact Report*</li><li>*Customer Authentication Strategic Leadership* team paper</li><li>*Innovation: Are we getting ahead of ourselves?*</li><li>*Members Directory*</li><li>*Myths and Realities of Payment Cards*</li><li>*Payments at the Point-of-Sale: Is evolution meeting stakeholder needs?*</li><li>Payments Business Magazine (4 articles)</li><li>*Privacy, Security and Fraud: Is there a balancing point?*</li><li>*Privacy: Risky Business?*</li><li>*Secure ID Report: Meeting the Needs of Governments and Citizens* (draft)</li><li>Secure-gov-id.com web site launched</li><li>*Where's the money in payment?*</li></ul>	<ul><li>*Canada vs the USA - The Contrast and Lessons for Mobile Payments* Cartes North America</li><li>*Canadians and Bitcoin* Financial Consumer Agency of Canada –</li><li>*Ecosystem Views: panel chair* Mobile Payment</li><li>*EMV leadership panel chair, speaker & EMV training* Mobile Payment Conference (Chicago)</li><li>*EMV training,* Mobile Payment Conference - instructor</li><li>EMV Workshop at the Mobile Payments Conference</li><li>*Legal & Regulatory Compliance Primer, speaker* Revolutionary Payment Solutions 2014 & Beyond</li><li>*Lessons Learned from EMV Migration Outside the US* ATM Mobile Innovation Summit, Washington DC,</li><li>*Merchants and Payments - panel moderator & Canada post EMV - speaker* ETA Transact 14</li><li>*Mobile Payment Ecosystem Views - track chair* Cartes North America</li><li>*Recent Payment Solution Developments and Market Trends panel moderator* Lexpert -</li><li>*The 800-LB. Gorilla: EMV Liability Shift is Looming - panel moderator* CNP</li></ul>

Key Additional Member Services	External Events (other)	Government Key Consultations
<ul><li>12 key international conferences offer discounts to members</li><li>130+ members participated in 40+ SLT meetings</li><li>ESD investigation starts</li><li>Secure-gov-id.com launched</li><li>The Home Depot EMV briefing, Atlanta</li><li>Members take advantage of $150+k in Cardware discounts</li><li>1 member customer appreciation day</li></ul>	<ul><li>Cartes Paris - Sesames Judge and ISCAN meeting</li><li>MAG conference</li><li>Money 20/20</li><li>Mobile Payments (Orlando)</li></ul>	<ul><li>Briefed 80 government officials from 6 federal government ministries on digital currencies and Bitcoin in particular (FCAC, Fintrac, OSFI, CRA, Department of Finance and Industry Canada).</li><li>Canadian Privacy Commissioner, consultation on private sector issues that would determine the key priorities for his office</li></ul>

and in the...

Canadian news

- MONERIS PAYD PRO EMPOWERS BUSINESSES TO ACCEPT PAYMENTS ON THE GO
- MONERIS SIGNS DEAL TO USE VERIFONE'S E-PAYMENT DEVICES
- MONERIS SOLUTIONS AND MILANO SOFTWARE OFFER NEW INTEGRATED PAYMENT SOLUTION
- MONERIS TO ENABLE UNIONPAY ACCEPTANCE FOR CANADIAN MERCHANTS
- NBS ACQUIRES EQUINOX PAYMENTS
- PAYFIRMA LAUNCHES AUTOMATED RECURRING BILLING FOR BUSINESSES
- PIVOTAL PAYMENTS EXPANDS ITS CANADIAN CARD ACCEPTANCE PLATFORM TO INCLUDE DISCOVER FINANCIAL SERVICES
- PROVINCE OF BRITISH COLUMBIA PARTNERS WITH SECUREKEY TO LAUNCH NEW BC SERVICES CARD; TRANSFORMING B.C. GOVERNMENT SERVICE DELIVERY WHILE DEMONSTRATING WORLD LEADING PRIVACY MODEL
- RBC RELEASES CANADIAN FACEBOOK MONEY TRANSFER APP
- RBC WALLET NOW AVAILABLE: FIRST MOBILE SOLUTION TO PROVIDE CANADIANS WITH THE CHOICE OF DEBIT OR CREDIT
- RFID CANADA UNVEILS EMV / NFC COMPLIANT PAYMENT READER FOR EXTREME CANADIAN CONDITIONS
- ROGERS LAUNCHES NFC-ENABLED MOBILE WALLET IN CANADA
- RONA AND THE AIR MILES REWARD PROGRAM SIGN MULTI-YEAR RENEWAL AGREEMENT
- ROYAL CANADIAN MINT LOOKING TO UNLOAD MINTCHIP PROGRAM
- ROYAL CANADIAN MINT SET TO DEMO DIGITAL CURRENCY
- SAY HELLO TO THE FUTURE WITH DESJARDINS MOBILE PAYMENT
- SECUREKEY CHOSEN BY ROYAL CANADIAN MINT TO AUTHENTICATE MINTCHIP DIGITAL CURRENCY CONSUMERS
- SECUREKEY CONCIERGE SERVICE SURPASSES ONE MILLION-CREDENTIAL MILESTONE
- TANGERINE ENABLES TOUCH ID, PLANS FOR VOICE BIOMETRICS
- TD AND MOVEN ANNOUNCE EXCLUSIVE CANADIAN AGREEMENT
- TD CANADA TRUST ANNOUNCED TD MOBILE PAYMENT, A SECURE PAYMENT SOLUTION THAT ALLOWS CUSTOMERS TO PAY FOR EVERYDAY PURCHASES WITH THEIR SMARTPHONES. AVAILABLE ON THE BELL, ROGERS, AND TELUS NETWORKS,
- TD LAUNCHES MOBILE DEPOSIT
- TD'S NEW ATMS TAKES CARE OF YOUR DEPOSITS IN A SNAP
- TENDER RETAIL'S MCM SOLUTION ALLOWS RETAILERS TO USE IPHONE 6 APPLE PAY FUNCTION
- TENDER RETAIL'S MCM SOLUTION ALLOWS RETAILERS TO USE IPHONE 6 APPLE PAY FUNCTION
- TIM HORTONS ADDS MOBILE PAYMENT OPTIONS
- TIM HORTONS AND CIBC ANNOUNCE AGREEMENT TO LAUNCH CO-BRANDED LOYALTY REWARDS VISA CREDIT CARD
- TIM HORTONS AND CIBC LAUNCH DOUBLE DOUBLE VISA CARD
- TORONTO AIRPORT RAIL LINE TO USE MOBILE TICKET SYSTEM
- TORONTONIANS CAN NOW PAY WITH THE PAYPAL MOBILE APP AT MORE THAN 50 CAFÉS AND RESTAURANTS
- UGO, THE WALLET FOR YOUR PHONE HAS ARRIVED
- WHY CANADA JUST MIGHT BE THE FUTURE OF U.S. MOBILE PAYMENTS

2013 Key highlights...

- ACT Canada takes members across the USA to help promote adoption of chip and pin in an effort to reduce cross border mag stripe fraud
- Through 4 member-initiated Strategic Leadership teams and other services, ACT Canada helped members focus on Mobile payment, customer authentication, point of sales issues and prepaid opportunities
- With members, the association publishes a report in the ESD experience in Canada and launches a secure ID report
- Over 120 members from around the world use ACT Canada Strategic Leadership teams to advance their goals

Metrics

- 15 member events / workgroups
- 4 EMV USA roadshow stops with member panelists
- 23 publications/reports/papers
- 15 speeches
- 14 government consultations / key interactions

The market...

- Issuers suffer from expensive cross border fraud as the US debates a move to chip
- Stakeholders struggle with the impacts of ESD and non-harmonized contactless certification
- Uncertainty of where to invest competes with ROI
- Secure ID advocates urge government to follow the lead of the financial sector in raising the bar with chip secured ID
- There are more partners and stakeholders involved in opportunities and issues adding complexity to both
- The future of e-wallets is questioned because of slow progress
- Research shows that only 6.8 % of boomers and 16.3% of bankers felt that a phone would replace the need to carry a physical wallet.

Board of Directors

Christian Ali	Dream Payments
Tracey Black	GFH Group
David Chaudhari	Ingenico Canada, Ltd.
Nino Di Teodoro	Di Teodoro Consulting Services
Owen Gingras	Walmart Canada
Lorna Johnson	Lorna Johnson
Catherine Johnston	ACT Canada
Doug Macdonald	MNP LLP
Karrie MacDonald	Gemalto
Wendy Maisey	ICC Solutions Ltd
Jennifer Passmore	Canadian Tire Financial Services
Didier Serra	SecureKey Technologies
Paul Zatychec	EWA-Canada Ltd.

ACT Canada notes of interest

- ACT commissions Secure ID report
- MAG (Merchant Advisory Group) and ACT Canada offer 2 for 1 membership for Canadian Retailers
- ACT Canada brings all the stakeholder groups together so that members can:
    - ✓ get the big picture
    - ✓ understand the nuances and
    - ✓ make informed decisions
  in a timely manner that saves on resources

...Filtering the Truth from Market Noise & Understanding Complex Issues

2013

Bringing members together and building an informed market

ACT Canada Member Events, Teams and Workgroups	Publications, Reports, Papers & Media	Speeches
▪ Annual General Meeting ▪ Awards Celebration 2013 ▪ Board Advisory Committee ▪ Cardware 2013: Payment Insights ▪ Cardware Connections networking event - leverage EMV profitably ▪ Cardware Connections networking event - the Dragons' Den ▪ Customer Authentication Strategic Leadership team ▪ Issues Alert team ▪ Merchant and Payment Networks Closed Door meetings ▪ Mobile Strategic Leadership Team ▪ Strategic Leadership team ▪ Point of Sale Strategic Leadership team ▪ President's Advisory Council ▪ Secure ID / Customer Authentication Strategic Leadership team ▪ Women in Payments Annual Networking meeting	▪ *5 myths about contactless payments* - Creditcards.com ▪ ACT news - driving insights (11 editions) ▪ *Cards in an evolving payments landscape* ▪ *Members Directory* ▪ *NFC in Canada: a stakeholder view* ▪ *North America: one payments market* ▪ Payments Business magazine articles (4) ▪ Secure ID report launch ▪ secure-gov-id.com launch ▪ *The ESD Experience in Canada* (editor)	▪ *Canada post EMV* ETA - (New Orleans) ▪ *Driving the Channel panel + International Development panel* Cardware 2013 ▪ *e-banking track chair* Cartes America ▪ *Emerging Mobile Payment Systems: Legal and Regulatory Risks - Current Market Outlook and Players: Where Are We Heading?* Osgoode Hall Law School ▪ *EMV migration Canada* AB Note ▪ EMV US Roadshow 2013 - Card Forum ▪ EMV US Roadshow 2013 - Cartes North America ▪ EMV US Roadshow 2013 - ETA ▪ EMV US Roadshow 2013 - MAG ▪ *EMV: what you need to know now* MAG ▪ *Enabling Infrastructure & Technology - The future of plastic in payment panel moderator* Money 20/20 ▪ *Fraud post EMV and what merchants need to look for and protect against* MAG webinar ▪ *Mobile Payment: needs of consumers and merchants* Canadian Wireless Telecommunications Association/Interac - NFC Payments Canada 2013 ▪ *Payment card fraud in an EMV environment panel – moderator* Card Forum ▪ *Regulatory horizon: problems and solutions* Lexpert Revolutionary Payment Solutions 2013 & Beyond: Legal & Regulatory Primer -

Key Additional Member Services	External Events (other)	Government Key Consultations & Interactions
<ul><li>International conferences offer discounts to ACT Canada members</li><li>Members meet with China Union Pay representatives from Shanghai</li><li>Members meet with the Ontario Ministry of Economic Development and Innovation</li><li>POS SLT continues work to identify the cause / control of ESD</li><li>Negotiated discounts to 7 major conferences</li><li>Members took advantage of more than $176,621 in Cardware discounts.</li></ul>	<ul><li>Cartes + ISCAN meeting</li><li>Cartes America</li><li>Connect ID (Washington)</li><li>Digital Money Unconference</li><li>Merchant Advisory Group (annual & mid-term) conferences</li><li>Payments Compliance in Canada conference</li></ul>	<ul><li>Advocacy with Ontario Liberal leadership candidates re chip security (7)</li><li>Queens Park Briefings for Smart health cards (6)</li><li>Ontario Ministry of Economic Development and Innovation consulted on the future of mobile apps and the Ontario Mobile Payment Sector Competitiveness Study</li></ul>

- AMERICAN EXPRESS CANADA SIGNS NEW MULTI-YEAR AGREEMENTS WITH AIMIA & AIR CANADA
- ATMIA CANADIAN CHAPTER FORMS GOVERNMENTAL RELATIONS COMMITTEE
- CANADA POST ADDED TO MIVA MERCHANT PLATFORM
- CANADA POST AND GOECART LAUNCH NEW E-COMMERCE COLLABORATION
- CANADA POST TEAMS UP WITH 3DCART TO PROVIDE STREAMLINED SHIPPING AND LOGISTICS SOLUTIONS FOR ONLINE RETAILERS
- CANADA POST TO LAUNCH DELIVERED TONIGHT SERVICE IN GTA
- CANADIAN SURE TAP ADDS ANDROID VERSION OF ITS MOBILE PAYMENT APP
- CANADIANS CAN NOW USE AMEX TO PAY VIA SQUARE
- CIBC ADDS MOBILE PAYMENTS SOLUTION FOR BUSINESS BANKING CLIENTS
- CIBC EXPANDS MOBILE PAYMENT APP TO BLACKBERRY Z10 AND Q10 SMARTPHONES
- COCA-COLA BRINGS FAST AND CONVENIENT REFRESHMENT TO CANADIANS WITH NEW INTERAC PAYMENT OPTION
- CREDIT UNIONS ARE FIRST IN CANADA TO LET USERS DEPOSIT ANYWHERE WITH SMARTPHONES
- DESJARDINS GROUP AND CRÉDIT MUTUEL-CIC GROUP LAUNCH INTERNATIONAL PAYMENT SOLUTIONS PARTNERSHIP
- DIRECTCASH PAYMENTS INC. ANNOUNCES $50 MILLION ACQUISITION OF THRESHOLD FINANCIAL TECHNOLOGIES INC.
- ENSTREAM TO ENABLE SECUREKEY AUTHENTICATION TECHNOLOGY ON BELL, ROGERS AND TELUS SMARTPHONES IN CANADA
- EWA-CANADA ACCREDITED BY VISA READY PARTNER PROGRAM TO PERFORM (MPOS) SOLUTIONS TESTING FOR CERTIFICATION
- FERTILE GROUND FOR MOBILE PAYMENTS IN CANADA
- FIRST INTERAC FLASH DEBIT TRANSACTIONS MADE FROM A MOBILE PHONE

- FISERV CERTIFIES GRG INTERNATIONAL ATMS FOR TRANSACTION PROCESSING IN CANADA
- FISERV DEBUTS INTERACTIVE MOBILE SALES SOLUTION TO HELP FINANCIAL INSTITUTIONS ACCELERATE REVENUE
- FOREVER 21 SETS THE TREND WITH INTERAC FLASH
- G&D CHOSEN BY CIBC AS TRUSTED SERVICE MANAGER FOR MOBILE PAYMENTS IN CANADA
- GROUNDBREAKING SECUREKEY MULTI-FACTOR AUTHENTICATION SERVICE SIMPLIFIES MOBILE APP SECURITY
- IBM TEAMS UP WITH ING DIRECT CANADA
- INGENICO AND TIMBEC PARTNER IN CANADA TO EXPAND SECURE INDOOR SELF-SERVICE PAYMENT ACCEPTANCE
- INTERAC DEBIT CARD FRAUD SKIMMING LOSSES PLUMMET TO LOWEST LEVEL ON RECORD
- MASTERCARD CANADA CALLING ALL DEVELOPERS TO MASTER THE CODE
- MASTERCARD MAKES IT EASY FOR CANADIANS TO TRAVEL SMARTER
- MASTERPASS DIGITAL WALLET LAUNCHES IN CANADA
- MATTEL AND WALMART CANADA OFFER HOLIDAY SHOPPERS TOYS ON THE GO
- MONERIS LAUNCHES PAYD PRO, CANADA'S FIRST DEBIT-ENABLED MOBILE PAYMENT SERVICE
- MONERIS PARTNERS WITH LUMINUS FINANCIAL
- MONERIS SOLUTIONS AND TOUCHBISTRO PARTNER TO PROVIDE INTEGRATED PAYMENT SOLUTION TO CANADIAN RESTAURANT MERCHANTS
- MONERIS SOLUTIONS PARTNERS WITH SECUREBUY, LEADING PROVIDER OF INNOVATIVE E-COMMERCE ANTI-FRAUD SOLUTIONS
- NEW MASTERCARD STUDY PUTS CANADA AMONG MOST ADVANCED IN THE WORLD FOR CASHLESS PAYMENTS

Canadian news

- NEXT IMPORTANT STEP TAKEN TO HELP INTERAC COMPETE IN A RAPIDLY CHANGING MARKET
- OBERTHUR TECHNOLOGIES AND STM EXTEND THEIR PARTNERSHIP FOR FOUR YEARS IN CANADIAN PUBLIC TRANSPORTATION AND CELEBRATE THE 5,000,000TH DISTRIBUTED CARD
- PAYMENT SOLUTIONS BY TENDER RETAIL, A DIVISION OF ACCEO SOLUTIONS, WILL SUPPORT THE EPAS RETAILER PROTOCOL
- PAYPAL, TOUCHBISTRO BRING SMARTPHONE PAYMENTS TO TORONTO RESTAURANTS
- PC FINANCIAL AND TD ANNOUNCE UGO - CANADA'S FIRST OPEN MOBILE WALLET
- RBC AND BELL BRING ANOTHER MOBILE PAYMENT SCHEME TO CANADA
- ROGERS BANK JOINS OBSI
- ROGERS COMMUNICATIONS TO LAUNCH LOYALTY REWARDS PROGRAM THIS YEAR
- ROGERS RECEIVES AUTHORIZATION TO LAUNCH LOYALTY CREDIT CARD
- ROGERS SURETAP SERVICE AVAILABLE FOR ANDROID, BLACKBERRY 10
- ROGERS TO DELIVER FIRST MOBILE WALLET FROM CANADIAN CARRIER
- SCOTIABANK RECEIVES VISA SERVICE QUALITY PERFORMANCE AWARDS
- SECUREKEY BRIIDGE.NET PLATFORM BRINGS TRUST TO MOBILE AND ONLINE TRANSACTIONS
- SECUREKEY CONCIERGE SERVICE ADDS ING DIRECT AS NEWEST TRUSTED SIGN-IN PARTNER
- SECUREKEY DIVESTS HARDWARE SECURITY TOKEN GROUP
- SECUREKEY PARTNER PROGRAM SPEEDS DEPLOYMENT OF EASY, SECURE ACCESS TO WEB AND MOBILE APPLICATIONS
- SIGNIFICANT STEP TAKEN TO BOLSTER INTERAC'S ABILITY TO COMPETE AND INNOVATE
- SUNOVA CREDIT UNION FIRST CREDIT UNION TO OFFER INTERAC FLASH(TM)
- TD BANK GROUP, AIMIA AND CIBC CONFIRM AGREEMENTS
- TD LAUNCHES TABLET BANKING APP FOR ANDROID
- THE INTERNATIONAL RETAIL USER GROUP CONGRATULATES HMV CANADA INC. AND SOLUTION PARTNER STJ RETAIL - WINNERS OF THE 2013 IRUG RETAIL INNOVATION AWARD
- VANCOUVER HOSTS BITCOIN'S ATM COMING OUT PARTY
- VISA JOINS BLACKBERRY MOBILE PHONE PAYMENT TECHNOLOGY
- AMERICAN EXPRESS CANADA SIGNS NEW MULTI-YEAR AGREEMENTS WITH AIMIA & AIR CANADA
- ATMIA CANADIAN CHAPTER FORMS GOVERNMENTAL RELATIONS COMMITTEE
- CANADA POST ADDED TO MIVA MERCHANT PLATFORM
- CANADA POST AND GOECART LAUNCH NEW E-COMMERCE COLLABORATION
- CANADA POST TEAMS UP WITH 3DCART TO PROVIDE STREAMLINED SHIPPING AND LOGISTICS SOLUTIONS FOR ONLINE RETAILERS
- CANADA POST TO LAUNCH DELIVERED TONIGHT SERVICE IN GTA
- CANADIAN SURE TAP ADDS ANDROID VERSION OF ITS MOBILE PAYMENT APP
- CANADIANS CAN NOW USE AMEX TO PAY VIA SQUARE
- CIBC ADDS MOBILE PAYMENTS SOLUTION FOR BUSINESS BANKING CLIENTS

2012 Key highlights...

- ACT Canada members join us on a US roadshow to help Americans make the move to EMV so that we can reduce costly cross-border mag stripe fraud
- Through 4 member initiated Strategic Leadership teams and other services, ACT Canada helped members focus on:
  - mobile payment, cyber-security, merchant strategy and prepaid / gift card opportunities
  - market issues and opportunities

Metrics

- 21 member events / workgroups
- 9 EMV USA roadshow stops with member panelists
- 28 publications / reports / papers
- 17 speeches / briefings
- 11 government consultations / key interactions

The market...

- A year of market change...
- The US moves from believing EMV will never come to their market, to skepticism about the announced dates
- Payments Review Task Force report is issued
- Passport Canada and the government of British Columbia follow the lead of the financial sector by adding chip security to ID
- Interac mandate for EMV compliant ATMs comes into effect
- Mobile dialogue shifts from what the technology can do to what the market will realistically do
- Questions payment stakeholders are asking

  Why didn't Apple clearly signal their preference for Bluetooth or NFC in their recent release?
  What should we think of the recent ISIS announcement that their wallet will be delayed?
  What does it mean when leading American merchants decide to establish their own wallet?
  Will the legal requirements to be compliant with the Durbin amendment impact stakeholders' ability to meet EMV requirements?
  When will we see relief from cross border fraud?

Board of Directors

Tracey Black	GFH Group
David Chaudhari	Ingenico Canada, Ltd.
Nino Di Teodoro	TD Canada Trust
Catherine Johnston	ACT Canada
Sharon MacAlpine	HSBC Credit Card Services
Karrie MacDonald	Gemalto
Susan MacKeown	Interac Association
Willis Morettin	Giesecke & Devrient
Susan Reynolds	Coinamatic Canada Inc.
Didier Serra	INSIDE Secure S.A.
Ryan van Orman	ATB Financial
Paul Zatvchec	EWA-Canada Ltd

ACT Canada notes of interest

- Surpasses 100 member milestone
- Launches USA EMV roadshow

2012

Bringing members together and building an informed market

ACT Canada Member Events, Teams and Workgroups	Publications, Reports, Papers & Media	Speeches
<ul><li>ACT Canada, Canadian Payments Association and Interac Association: 2012 Mobile Proximity Payments Forum</li><li>Annual General Meeting</li><li>Awards Celebration 2012</li><li>Board Advisory Committee</li><li>Cardware 2012: Payment Insights</li><li>Cardware Connection Networking event: Supply chain security</li><li>Cardware Connections Networking event - MCX</li><li>Cyber Security for Payments Strategic Leadership team</li><li>EMV (US) roadmap meeting</li><li>EMV for the US Strategic Leadership team</li><li>EMV Stakeholders Group (US - MAG) launched</li><li>ID Strategic Leadership team</li><li>Issues Management team</li><li>Merchant and Payment Networks closed door meetings</li><li>Merchant Workshop (Niagara)</li><li>Mobile Strategic Leadership team</li><li>POS Strategic Leadership team</li><li>Prepaid and Gift cards Strategic Leadership team</li><li>Prepaid, Gift Cards and Stored Value Products workshop (with Payments Business)</li><li>President's Advisory Council</li><li>Secure ID Strategic Leadership team</li></ul>	<ul><li>*ACT Canada Quick Reference Guide for Prepaid Card Programs*</li><li>ACT news - driving insights (11 editions)</li><li>ACTion e-bulletin, MasterCard Announces EMV plans for the US</li><li>*Best EMV practices*</li><li>Canadian news sent quarterly to members of ACT Canada, the Smart Card Alliance, Eurosmart, the Smart Card Forum of China, the French Association of Card Manufacturers and Service Bureau, EESTEL and Global Platform via ISCAN</li><li>*Consumer reaction to CHIP and PIN in Canada* for the American Bankers Association Law Committee</li><li>*Members Directory*</li><li>*Mobile SLT report*</li><li>*Payments.com interview*</li><li>Quarterly articles for Payments Business Magazine</li><li>*USA EMV best practices for retailers*</li><li>www.emv-usa.com launched</li></ul>	<ul><li>*Canada EMV Report, Opportunities for the Global and Chinese Mobile Payments Market panel moderator & co-host opening remarks* 2nd World IC Summit - (Beijing)</li><li>Canadian Payments Association / Interac / ACT Canada Mobile event</li><li>*e-business track chair* Cartes North America</li><li>EMV US Roadshow - Cartes America - panel</li><li>EMV US Roadshow ATM Debit & Prepaid Forum 2012 - EMV workshop</li><li>EMV US Roadshow Card Forum - panel</li><li>EMV US Roadshow ICMA Technology Summit - panel</li><li>EMV US roadshow Merchant Advisory Group annual conference- *Are We Ready for Chip and PIN? Panel moderator*</li><li>EMV US roadshow Merchant Advisory Group mid-year workshop</li><li>EMV US Roadshow MidWest Acquirers' Association - panel</li><li>EMV US Roadshow Smart Card Alliance Payments - Workshop</li><li>EMV US Roadshow Southeast Acquirers' Association - panel</li><li>*Keynote Plenary Panel Merchants and Processors Panel on EMV Preparations in the US – moderator* Smart Card Alliance Payments Summit</li><li>*Market Update* Cardware Connections</li><li>*Privacy and Security Issues* Revolutionary Payment Solutions 2013 and beyond: legal and regulatory</li></ul>

- compliance primer (Toronto)
- *Stakeholders view of EMV and why merchants are so important* IRUG
- *The evolving Canadian Payments Landscape* CAMA (Niagara Falls)

Key Additional Member Services	External Events (other)	Government Key Consultations & Interactions
<ul><li>Consulting services for the Mohawk of Akwesasne – Secure ID Card</li><li>EMV SME at NRF (Ingenico booth)</li><li>EMV Stakeholder meetings (3)</li><li>Gemalto Technology Day</li><li>Invited 2 members to meet with China UnionPay in Shanghai</li><li>ISCAN quarterly news from around the world</li><li>Members have increased control of their online directory listings</li><li>Members save $144k+ in discounts at Cardware</li><li>Members receive discounts at Mobile Money Canada, Cartes and the Smart Card Alliance Government show</li></ul>	<ul><li>Cartes (Paris)</li><li>Canadian Institute Prepaid Conference</li><li>China UnionPay meeting - Shanghai</li></ul>	<ul><li>Mohawk of Akwesasne – multiple presentations on a Secure ID card. This project involved Indian and Northern Affairs and the US Department of Homeland Security</li><li>Launched an ombudsman's investigation into health card fraud (Ontario red & white Cards)</li><li>Secure ID Awareness briefings with Ontario government ministries (8)</li></ul>

- A NEW CHAPTER IN CONVENIENCE: INTERAC FLASH AT INDIGO
- A PERFECT COMBO - INTERAC FLASH AT MCDONALD'S IN CANADA
- ACONITE & PAYMOBILE PARTNER FOR EMV PREPAID CARD ISSUANCE PROGRAM MANAGEMENT IN CANADA
- AEROPLAN AND IMPERIAL OIL RENEW AGREEMENT
- CANADA LEADS THE WAY IN ADOPTION OF MASTERCARD CONTACTLESS PAYMENTS
- CANADA POST DELIVERS INNOVATION WITH NEXT GENERATION OF EPOST
- CANADA'S PAYMENT SYSTEMS NEED MOBILE BOOST, FEDERAL REVIEW ARGUES
- CANADIAN CARRIERS TO LAUNCH NFC PAYMENTS 'WITHIN SIX MONTHS'
- CANADIAN GOVERNMENT TO EXTEND PLASTIC CARD CODE TO MOBILE PAYMENTS – MEMBERS ONLY STORY
- CANADIAN NEXUS MEMBERS ELIGIBLE FOR TSA PRE CHECK
- CANADIAN SOLUTION PROVIDER OFFERS INSTANT CARD ISSUANCE USING MULTOS
- CHASE AND MARRIOTT REWARDS LAUNCH THE ONLY HOTEL REWARDS CREDIT CARD IN CANADA WITH NO FOREIGN CURRENCY TRANSACTION CHARGES
- CHASE LAUNCHES THE AMAZON.CA REWARDS VISA CARD IN CANADA
- CHIP TECHNOLOGY HELPING IN THE FIGHT AGAINST INTERAC DEBIT CARD FRAUD
- CIBC & ROGERS UNVEIL THE FUTURE OF MOBILE PAYMENTS IN CANADA
- CIBC CONTINUES ITS LEADERSHIP IN MOBILE FINANCIAL SERVICES WITH THE LAUNCH OF NEW TEXT MESSAGE ALERTS
- CIBC INTRODUCES A MOBILE BANKING APP DESIGNED SPECIFICALLY FOR IPAD USERS
- CIBC, ROGERS COMPLETE MOBILE CREDIT CARD TRANSACTION
- CITY OF TORONTO LAUNCHES CITY SERVICES BENEFIT CARD

- CPI CANADA FACILITY RECEIVES ISO CERTIFICATION
- DATACARD GROUP PROVIDES ENHANCED CARD DELIVERY FOR QUEBEC'S DRIVER'S LICENSE AND ID PROGRAM MODULAR
- DIRECT CASH PAYMENTS INC. ANNOUNCES INITIATIVE WITH VISA CANADA TO HELP MAKE ATM
- TRANSACTIONS MORE ACCESSIBLE FOR VISITORS TO CANADA
- DISCOVER IMPLEMENTS 2013 EMV MANDATE IN U.S., CANADA AND MEXICO
- ENSTREAM LP TO ENABLE SECURE MOBILE PAYMENTS IN CANADA – MEMBERS ONLY STORY
- EVERLINK INTRODUCES - MERCHANT ACQUIRING PROGRAM

Canadian news

- FINANCIAL INDUSTRY ANNOUNCES GUIDELINES FOR MOBILE PAYMENTS IN CANADA
- FREE CREDIT UNION MOBILE APP NOW AVAILABLE
- GIESECKE & DEVRIENT EXTENDS CANADIAN REACH WITH NEW PERSONALIZATION BUREAU IN QUEBEC
- GOOGLE CALLS CANADA 'ONE OF OUR BIG BETS,' LOOKS TO GROW FURTHER HERE IN 2012 - MEMBERS ONLY
- HARPER GOVERNMENT UNVEILS NEW EPASSPORT
- HOME TRUST TEAMS UP WITH MASTERCARD CANADA
- IMPARK SPEEDS AHEAD WITH VISA PAYWAVE & VISA DEBIT TECHNOLOGY
- INTERAC FLASH IS THE NEWEST HIT AT HMV CANADA
- INTERAC FLASH NOW AVAILABLE AT TIM HORTONS
- INTERAC FLASH ON THE MENU AT EXTREME BRANDZ
- INTERAC FLASH PROVIDES ESSO CUSTOMERS WITH MORE CONVENIENCE
- INTERAC FLASH(TM) GOES TO THE MOVIES WITH CINEPLEX

- INTERAC ONLINE CLEARED FOR TAKEOFF WITH AIR CANADA
- LAUNCH OF THE COLLIS MERCHANT TEST SUITE FOR US AND CANADIAN MARKETS
- MASTERCARD ANNOUNCES PAYPASS WALLET SERVICES
- METRO GROCERY CHAIN ADOPTS VISA CONTACTLESS PAYMENTS
- MOBILE PRIVACY A CONCERN AMONG CANADIAN SHOPPERS
- MONERIS AND SEMAFONE PARTNER TO PROVIDE SECURE CONTACT CENTRE EXPERIENCE
- MONERIS OFFERS A NEW MOBILE CASH REGISTER EXPERIENCE
- NEW SMARTPHONE APP FOR MOVIE LOVERS TO LAUNCH THIS SUMMER IN TORONTO – MEMBERS ONLY ACCESS
- NOW ARRIVING: SCOTIABANK AMERICAN EXPRESS TRAVEL REWARDS CARDS LAND IN CANADA
- NOW SERVING...VISA AT TIM HORTONS
- OBERTHUR TECHNOLOGIES TO OPEN SERVICE CENTER IN CANADA FOR GROWING EMV, NFC AND ID MARKETS
- PAY IN A FLASH AT HARVEY'S AND SWISS CHALET
- RBC INTRODUCES VIRTUAL VISA DEBIT
- ROGERS COMMUNICATIONS SELECTS GEMALTO TO SECURE MOBILE NFC PAYMENT SOLUTIONS
- ROYAL CANADIAN MINT ANNOUNCES DIGITAL CURRENCY
- ROYAL CANADIAN MINT ANNOUNCES WINNERS IN THE MINTCHIP(TM) DEVELOPER CHALLENGE
- SEARS CANADA AMONG FIRST CANADIAN RETAILERS TO LAUNCH ONLINE POINTS REDEMPTION FEATURE
- SEARS FINANCIAL SAYS FAREWELL TO FOREIGN CURRENCY TRANSACTION CHARGES FOR OVER TWO MILLION CANADIANS
- SECUREKEY LAUNCHES ONLINE AUTHENTICATION SERVICE FOR GOVERNMENT OF CANADA
- SQUARE CARD READERS NOW SOLD IN MORE THAN 250 RETAIL STORES IN CANADA, INCLUDING APPLE AND BEST BUY – MEMBERS ONLY STORY
- SQUARE LAUNCHES IN CANADA – MEMBERS ONLY STORY
- TARGET TO OFFER 5% SAVINGS EVERY DAY IN CANADA WITH REDCARD REWARDS
- TD BANK GROUP TO ACQUIRE TARGET'S U.S. CREDIT CARD PORTFOLIO AND ENTER INTO A SEVEN-YEAR PROGRAM AGREEMENT
- TD UNVEILS CANADA'S MOST COMPREHENSIVE DEBIT CARD
- TORONTONIANS HAVE AN APPETITE FOR A NEW KIND OF FOOD REVOLUTION: CASHLESS
- TSYS PREPS FOR NFC WITH CIBC
- TTC TO TRY MOBILE PRESTO PAYMENTS THIS SUMMER
- UNIV. OF TORONTO RESEARCH TEAM DEVELOPS MOBILE ID PROTECTION APP – MEMBERS ONLY
- VISA DEBIT TAKES FLIGHT WITH AIR CANADA
- VISA DEBIT TAKES OFF AT WESTJET
- WESTERN UNION SIGNS AGREEMENT WITH ACXSYS CORPORATION TO OFFER EXPANDED ONLINE ACCOUNT-BASED MONEY TRANSFER SERVICE TO FINANCIAL INSTITUTION CUSTOMERS IN CANADA

2011 Key highlights...

- An unprecedented number of members ask for special services as the market enters the post EMV rollout stage
- Through 6 member-initiated Strategic Leadership teams and other services, ACT Canada helped members focus on:
  - mobile payment, cyber-security, merchant strategy and prepaid / gift card opportunities, market issues and secure chip
  - market issues and opportunities

Metrics

- 19 member events / workgroups
- 27 publications / reports / papers
- 16 speeches / briefings
- 5 government consultations / key interactions

The market...

- EMV: Liability shift for MasterCard and Visa occurred in Canada at the end of Q1.
- US remains skeptical about EMV but starts to ask questions
- ACT Canada plans a US roadshow with members to help Americans move to EMV, to reduce costly cross-border mag stripe fraud
- Passport Canada considers a 10 year passport
- The Privacy Commissioner urges the industry to "bake privacy into NFC chips now"
- NFC mobile payment and contactless cards are a strong market focus
- Data encryption is seen as the new security solution
- Canadian stakeholders start to encounter ESD problems
- British Columbia announces smart (chip) CareCards
- When will we be able to close the door on mag stripe vulnerabilities?
- Interac announces that Flash will debut 2011 and Visa launches Visa debit
- Seventy-four percent of American and Canadian consumers said they don't feel they're receiving a benefit from sharing personal information with marketers
- NFC, m-commerce and micro-payment are focal points

Board of Directors

Tracey Black	GFH Group
David Chaudhari	Ingenico Canada, Ltd.
Nino Di Teodoro	Citi Cards Canada Inc.
Sharon Fisk	ATB Financial
Catherine Johnston	ACT Canada
Sharon MacAlpine	HSBC Credit Card Services
Willis Morettin	Giesecke & Devrient
Susan Reynolds	Coinamatic Canada Inc.
Didier Serra	INSIDE Contactless
Allen Wright	Interac Association
Paul Zatychec	EWA-Canada Ltd

ACT Canada notes of interest

It was a banner year...

- Exceeded our new member target by 46%.
- New growth primarily from organizations that want to work with other stakeholders in the emerging payments space
- Members can be found through 379 category affiliations on the ACT Canada site directory
- 99 members saved a total of $118,402 on registration at Cardware 2011
- 79 members have hotlinks from our site to theirs
- 50 members (represented by 80 staff) participate in Strategic Leadership teams
- 38 members had speaker / panelist / moderator spots at Cardware 2011

2011

Bringing members together and building an informed market

ACT Canada Member Events Teams & Workgroups	Publications, Reports, Papers & Media	Speeches, Briefings
- 5 members had EMV – US speaking opportunities at the Smart Card Alliance annual meeting, arranged by ACT - Annual Awards Celebration - Annual General Meeting - Board Advisory Committee members joined board meetings - Cardware 2011: Payment Insights (Niagara Falls) - Cardware Connections networking event: Securing the Supply Chain - Cyber Security for Payments Strategic Leadership team (with ITAC) - EMV for the US workshop - EMV road show committee was formed - Issues Alert team - Merchant Strategic Leadership team - Merchants and Payment Networks – closed door sessions - Mobile Commerce Strategic Leadership team - Prepaid Cards Strategic Leadership team - Prepaid day (with Global Prepaid Exchange) - President's Advisory Council - Secure Chip SLT (partnered with ITAC) - SLT chairs met together in Q1 - Stakeholder Issues meeting	- ACT news - driving insights (11 editions) - ACTion e-bulletin announcing Visa's plan to accelerate EMV in the US - *Canada Puts Down Chip Card Roots* – Digital Transactions interview - Canadian news sent quarterly to members of ACT Canada, the Smart Card Alliance, Eurosmart, the Smart Card Forum of China, the French Association of Card Manufacturers and Service Bureau, EESTEL and Global Platform via ISCAN - *Chip and PIN – next steps* - emv-usa.com launched - *Credit Card Tricks* Macleans interview - *Members Directory* - *Mobile report* from the Strategic Leadership team - Payments Business Magazine quarterly articles - *Prepaid Card report* from the Strategic Leadership team - *Protecting Our Own Identities: A Call to ACTion* - *Retailers, EMV and 2015* - *Secure ID report* from the Strategic Leadership team	- *"Questions you should ask your staff"* dealing with rapid and extensive changes to the payments market Payments Business Senior bankers Breakfast Briefing and Networking - *Canadians Discuss the EMV Experiences - panel moderator* Smart Card Alliance Annual General meeting (Chicago) - *EMV and Fraud panel* Card Forum - *EMV discussions* MAG conference (Dallas) - *EMV in the US* Cardware 2011 - *EMV panel moderator* ICMA Technology Summit (Chicago) - *EMV Session SME* Merchant Advisory Group (MAG) - *Fraud after EMV* Ombudsman Banking Services and Investments – - *Fraud after EMV panel* Card Forum (Miami) - *Fraud and Security* ITAC Cyber Security Forum - Keynote *EMV Canadian Style* EMVCo Technical Advisors Meeting (Montreal) - *Mobile Payment Applications & Services panel moderator* Mobile Money Canada - *Payment Innovation! What Are Emerging Countries Doing Differently?* Executive International Roundtable: - *Social Media and the Financial Sector – panel moderator* RBC & The Access Group - *Social Media panel moderator* Payment Innovations - *The evolution of payments* Canadian Urban Transportation Association

Key Additional Member Services	External Events (other)	Government Key Consultations
- 1 member has us facilitate a partner event - 1 member had us facilitate a technology day - 1 member requests a strategy briefing - 11 members participate on the Board of Directors - 18 members participate on the President's Advisory Council - 21 members save a total of $35,650 on exhibiting at Cardware 2011 - 3 members (7 invited) give Card Not Present demos at Cardware 2011 facilitated by ACT Canada - 3 members bring issues to the Issues Alert team - 38 members have speaker / panelist / moderator spots at Cardware - 4 members participate on the Board Advisory Committee (BAC) - 4 members request market briefings - 5 members (7 invited) had EMV – US speaking opportunities at the Smart Card Alliance annual meeting, arranged by ACT - 5 members highlight their expertise by answering the questions on the EMV-USA web site(all members invited to submit answers) - 50 members (represented by 80 staff) participate in Strategic Leadership teams - 79 members have hotlinks from our sites to theirs (out of 95) - 99 members save a total of $118,402 on registration at Cardware 2011	- Cartes - Sesames Judge + ISCAN meeting - Cartes North America program committee - Million Acts of Payment Innovation information sessions from the Access Group - Prepaid and Gift Cards (with the Global Prepaid Exchange) - Smart Card Alliance Mobile and Transit Payment Summit	- Mohawk of Akwesasne – ACT Canada developed the RFP for a secure tax exemption identification system. This project involved the Ontario Ministry of Finance, The Canadian Revenue Agency, Indian and Northern Affairs and the US Department of Homeland Security - Passport Canada roundtable on 10 year passport

Key Additional Member Services (continued)

- Members can be found through 379 category affiliations on the ACT Canada site directory
- Members are invited to participate in various "Million Acts of payment innovation" information sessions run by the Access Group
- OBSI requests a "Fraud after EMV" briefing

and in the...

- A FIRST IN CANADA: DESJARDINS LAUNCHES END-TO-END DATA ENCRYPTION SOLUTION FOR CREDIT CARD PAYMENT
- A PROMISING PARTNERSHIP BETWEEN YESPAY AND TECHRIDER OFFERS AN INTEGRATED EMV PAYMENT SOLUTION TO CANADIAN STORES
- AMEX BANK OF CANADA LAUNCHES NEW B2B PAYMENTS SOLUTION
- BAKE PRIVACY INTO NFC CHIPS NOW, PRIVACY COMMISSIONER SAYS
- BC'S NEW ID CARDS GO BEYOND HEALTH CARE
- BMO FIRST MAJOR CANADIAN BANK TO ROLL OUT 'TAP AND GO' PAYMENT SOLUTION FOR MOBILE PHONES
- CANADA READIES EPASSPORT LAUNCH
- CANADA'S ROGERS PLANNING NFC MOBILE-PAYMENT LAUNCH
- CANADIAN ANDROID USERS TARGETED BY 'EXPENSIVE TEXTS' MALWARE
- CANADIAN BANK NOTE AWARDED CANADIAN EPASSPORT CONTRACT
- CANADIAN BOOKSTORE CHAIN ADOPTS CONTACTLESS PAYMENTS
- CANADIANS LEAD THE MOBILE TECHNOLOGY DRIVE
- CAPITAL ONE CANADA EXPANDS INTO QUEBEC
- CHASE PAYMENTECH HELPS PROTECT MERCHANTS AND CONSUMERS FROM PAYMENT CARD FRAUD AND DATA THEFT - LAUNCH OF SAFETECHSM ENCRYPTION IN CANADA
- COINAMATIC CANADA INC. ANNOUNCES ACQUISITION OF VENDA WASH
- COLLIS RELEASES TEST TOOLS APPROVED BY AMERICAN EXPRESS FOR THE CANADIAN MARKET
- COLLIS TERMINAL FUNCTIONAL TEST TOOL (FTT) QUALIFIED BY INTERAC ASSOCIATION FOR DUAL INTERFACE (DI)
- ELAVON CERTIFIES HYPERCOM'S SPOS32 EMV ON OPTIMUM PAYMENT SYSTEMS FOR CANADA
- GAUGE MOBILE, NEWAD LAUNCH NFC-ENABLED ADS IN CANADA

- GLOBAL PAYMENTS INTRODUCES INGENICO ICT250 READER TO CANADA
- HMV HITS A HIGH NOTE WITH VISA PAYWAVE IN-STORE AND VISA DEBIT ONLINE
- ICCSIMTMAT APPROVED BY AMERICAN EXPRESS FOR THE CANADIAN MARKET FOR TERMINAL CERTIFICATION
- INTERAC FLASH TO BE ACCEPTED AT PETRO-CANADA LOCATIONS ACROSS CANADA
- LATEST IN VISA PAYMENT TECHNOLOGY ROLLS OUT AT SEARS CANADA - SEARS CANADA TO ENABLE VISA DEBIT AND VISA PAYWAVE FOR CANADIAN SHOPPERS FROM COAST-TO-COAST
- MASTERCARD EXPANDS PAYPASS IN CANADA WITH CIBC
- MASTERCARD PAYPASS CONTACTLESS PAYMENT TECHNOLOGY INTRODUCED AT OVERWAITEA FOOD GROUP STORES

Canadian news

- MCDONALD'S CANADA INTRODUCES MASTERCARD PAYPASS CONTACTLESS PAYMENT TECHNOLOGY POINT-OF-SALE PAYMENT TERMINALS AVAILABLE AT MORE THAN 1,400 RESTAURANT LOCATIONS NATIONALLY
- PASSPORT CANADA SET TO INTRODUCE SECURITY-ENHANCED PASSPORT
- PERSON-TO-PERSON PAYMENTS GO MOBILE WITH INTERAC E-TRANSFER
- RIM ANNOUNCES FIRST NFC-ENABLED BLACKBERRYS
- RIM GOES NFC FOR SOCIAL MEDIA SHARING
- RIM PLANS 'BIG PUSH' FOR NFC-ENABLED BLACKBERRY APPS -
- ROGERS SEEKS BANK LICENCE - ACCESS
- SCOTIABANK CARDHOLDERS CAN NOW PAY SECURELY FOR ON-THE-GO PURCHASES WITH VISA PAYWAVE
- SCOTIABANK UNVEILS SCENE SCOTIACARD WITH INTERAC FLASH
- SECUREKEY TECHNOLOGIES INC. TO POWER THE GOVERNMENT OF CANADA'S NEW ONLINE AUTHENTICATION SERVICE

- TD BANK GROUP TO ACQUIRE MBNA CANADA'S CREDIT CARD BUSINESS
- VANCOUVER'S NEW FARE SYSTEM PAVES THE WAY FOR CONTACTLESS BANK CARD TRANSIT PAYMENTS
- VISA LAUNCHES V.ME DIGITAL WALLET
- VISA PAYWAVE NOW AVAILABLE AT 43 TORONTO PARKING AUTHORITY PARKING LOTS
- VISA'S CONTACTLESS TECHNOLOGY NOW AVAILABLE AT PARTICIPATING MCDONALD'S RESTAURANTS ACROSS CANADA
- YESPAY'S FIRST LIVE RETAIL CHAIN WITH FIRST DATA IN CANADA!

2010 Key highlights...

- Through 7 member-initiated Strategic Leadership teams and other services, ACT Canada helped members focus on:
  - cyber security, government, identity management, issues alerts, merchant, mobile and prepaid issues and opportunities
  - market issues and opportunities

Metrics

- 21 member events / workgroups
- 36 publications / reports / papers
- 13 speeches, briefings
- 12 government consultations / key interactions

The market...

- The Minister of Finance Code of Conduct for the credit and debit card industry in Canada comes into effect in August
- Canadian government announced the formation of a Task Force for the Payments System Review to help guide the evolution of the payments system in Canada
- As Canada rolls out chip, EMVCo reports that over one billion EMV cards and 15.4 million EMV terminals are active globally as of September 1, 2010 and that 36% of total cards and 65% of total terminals in circulation are now based on the EMV standard.
- Canadian EMV liability shift date is extended to early 2011
- With EMV infrastructure substantially rolled out, stakeholders are looking at how to leverage that investment. Mobile commerce, contactless, dual interfaces and new form factors are of interest to a broad group of stakeholders.
- Commissioner of the Competition Bureau announces the long awaited decision regarding Interac's request to vary consent order
- Industry Canada held roundtable discussions on "Protecting the Online Marketplace" as a part of the consultations for the Digital Economy Strategy.
- EMV infrastructure is substantially rolled out.

Board of Directors

Richard Adamson	*Coinamatic Canada Inc.*
Nino Di Teodoro	*Citi Cards Canada Inc.*
Sharon Fisk	*ATB Financial*
Catherine Johnston	*ACT Canada*
Sharon MacAlpine	*HSBC Credit Card Services*
Susan Reynolds	Coinamatic Canada Inc
Didier Serra	*INSIDE Contactless*
Allen Wright	*Interac Association*
Paul Zatychec	*EWA-Canada Ltd*

ACT Canada notes of interest

- The American Bankers Association Law Committee asks ACT Canada to provide information on EMV, principally in regards to consumer reaction to CHIP and PIN in Canada.
- Membership grows by 31%
- Payment stakeholders turned to ACT Canada to get both information and insights.

2010

Bringing members together and building an informed market

ACT Canada Member Events, Teams and Workgroups	Publications, Reports, Papers & Media	Speeches, Briefings
<ul><li>Annual General Meeting</li><li>Awards Celebration 2010</li><li>Board Advisory Committee</li><li>Cardware 2010: Payment Insights (Niagara Falls)</li><li>Cardware Connections - Payments System Review Board</li><li>Cardware Connections fall networking meeting - Mobile</li><li>Cyber Security Strategic Leadership team</li><li>EMV 101 workshop</li><li>EMV for the US (Niagara workshop)</li><li>Identity Management Strategic Leadership team (public/private sectors)</li><li>Issues Alert team formed</li><li>Merchant Strategic Leadership team</li><li>Mobile Strategic Leadership team (report at Cardware)<ul><li>4 subgroups</li><li>43 documents</li></ul></li><li>Prepaid Strategic Leadership team</li><li>President's Advisory Council</li><li>Stakeholders' issues meeting</li><li>Task Force for the Payments System Review, Stakeholder meeting</li><li>Women In Payments charity golf round</li><li>Women in Payments fall networking</li><li>Women In Payments spring networking</li><li>Women in Payments workgroup</li></ul>	<ul><li>*2010: Canadian Payment trends, questions and observations*</li><li>ACT news - driving insights (11 editions)</li><li>*Best EMV practices*</li><li>*Chip and PIN – the next steps*</li><li>*Contactless PIA and design tools* (with IPC/O)</li><li>Euromonitor</li><li>*Information versus insights*</li><li>International Smart Card Associations Network newsletter; bringing a world of news to our members – launched January</li><li>*Member Directory*</li><li>*Merchant and EMV: Best Practices*</li><li>*Preparing Merchants for the Future of Payments*</li><li>*Merchant questions asked and answered* (emvcanada website)</li><li>*Mobile Blueprint*</li><li>*Ontario Smart Card project review*</li><li>Over 25 key stakeholder organizations including financial institutions, telecommunication companies and suppliers form ACT Canada's Mobile Strategic Leadership team and produce *10 documents, including a list of market inhibitors, a watch list of potential regulatory influences and other pertinent information.*</li><li>Payments Business article</li><li>*Payments: fundamental change*</li></ul>	<ul><li>*Canada: a market in flux* Gift and Prepaid Retreat</li><li>Cartes - Sesames Judge + ISCAN meeting</li><li>*Chip panel* PCC Payment Card Security Conference</li><li>*Developing a Trusted Cyber Infrastructure for Canadians* Identity, Privacy and Security Institute (U of T) 2010</li><li>*EMV Best Practices for Merchants* Merchant Advisory Group (MAG) -</li><li>*EMV Canada and the USA: an exercise in stakeholder management* American Bankers Association Conference</li><li>*EMV Canada and the USA: an exercise in stakeholder management* Federal Reserve Bank of Philadelphia: Payments Security</li><li>*EMV for the US*</li><li>EMV Workshop MAG (Dallas)</li><li>Industry Canada Digital Economy roundtable participant.</li><li>*Mobile Myths and Realities –* (Mobile SLT) Cardware</li><li>*Prepaid in Canada* Prepaid Conference:</li><li>*Top 10 questions related to retail payments* IRUG - Retail Payment Strategies and Best Practices (San Antonio)</li></ul>

Key Additional Member Services	External Events (other)	Government Key Consultations
• Board Advisory Committee is launched • Developed RFP for a secure tax exemption identification system - members responded • Discounts on Mobile Payment Opportunities in Canada – IDC research • Discounts on Nilson Report • Gemalto Education Day • ISCAN newsletter distributed to members • Issues Alert team starts to look at ESD and 2 other issues • Mohawk of Akwesasne consulting services – Secure Tax Exemption Card, Privacy Impact Assessment, Secure ID Card • OBSI briefings • PIN management RFP • Searchable member directory added to web site • STJ Retail - EMV Best Practices and Lesson Learned: Retailers Perspective webinar • STJ webinar – EMV in the USA	• Cartes – North America • Cartes – Sesames judge • CPA Panorama • ISCAN meeting • ITAC cyber security group • ITAC ePayment Security Task Force • Merchant Advisory Group (MAG) • Payments Business Breakfast Briefing • Smart Card Alliance Annual Conference • Smart Card Alliance Payments Summit	• Department of Finance Task Force for the Payments System Review consulted ACT Canada on the future of the Canadian payments system • First Nations Status Card meeting • Industry Canada Digital Economy: protecting the online marketplace - roundtable participation • Ontario Government review of card projects • Ontario Ministry of Finance, The Canadian Revenue Agency, Indian and Northern Affairs and the US Department of Homeland Security consultations on indigenous passports. • Passport Canada - invited participant for Passport Services Stakeholder Consultation (Ottawa) • Province of Ontario asks us to debrief them on previous attempts to move to chip based health cards • Royal Canadian Mint – digital currency • Treasury Board discussions on public / private sector involvement in ID management

and in the...

- CANADIAN EMV LIABILITY SHIFT DATE EXTENSION TO EARLY 2017
- CANADIAN GOVERNMENT TABLES NEW CODE OF CONDUCT FOR PAYMENT CARDS
- COMMISSIONER OF COMPETITION ANNOUNCES DECISION RE. INTERAC'S REQUEST TO VARY CONSENT ORDER
- 100,000 TD CUSTOMERS HAVE AN "APP"ETITE FOR MOBILE. TD EXPANDS MOBILE OFFERING WITH BLACKBERRY AND ANDROID APPS.
- 2 NEW CANADIAN MOBILE PAYMENT REPORTS AVAILABLE FROM ACT CANADA.
- ACT CANADA ANNOUNCES NEW ISSUES ALERT TEAM.
- ALBERTA LOOKS AT BIOMETRIC IDS FOR HOMELESS.
- AMEX CANADA SETS OCTOBER 2012 EMV LIABILITY-SHIFT.
- CANADA POST TO INTRODUCE PIN SERVICES IN POST OFFICES.
- CANADA TO GET EPASSPORTS IN 2012.
- CANADA'S BIOMETRIC PASSPORT PROMISE REVIVED.
- CANADA'S SURCHARGE-FREE ATM NETWORK MIGRATES TO EMV.
- CANADIAN MOBILE OPERATORS 'PLAN TO INTRODUCE NFC HANDSETS WITHIN THE YEAR'.
- CIBC LAUNCHES MOBILE BANKING FOR IPHONE.
- EDMONTON EYES ALL-IN-ONE SMART CARD SYSTEM.
- GEMALTO EXPANDS CANADIAN PERSONALIZATION FACILITY FOR ENHANCED EMV MIGRATION SERVICES.
- GLOBAL PAYMENTS FIRST TO BRING VERIFONE PAYWARE MOBILE FOR IPHONE TO CANADA.

Canadian news

- INTERAC CERTIFIES NEW INGENICO PAYMENT DEVICE AS SAFEST FOR UNATTENDED & PETRO PAYMENT TERMINALS.
- INTERAC LAUNCHES CONTACTLESS TERMINAL INTEROPERABILITY & CONFIDENCE TEST PACKAGE.
- INTERAC DEBIT ON THE MENU AT TIM HORTONS.
- INTERAC FLASH INTRODUCED TO MARKET.
- INTERAC OFFERS ATM ISOS ALTERNATIVES TO COMPLY WITH CHIP MIGRATION.
- MAJOR CANADIAN PAYMENT PROCESSORS SUPPORT AMERICAN EXPRESS CHIP CARDS.
- MOBILE MARKET BRIEF RELEASED BY ACT CANADA'S MOBILE STRATEGIC LEADERSHIP TEAM.
- NBS TECHNOLOGIES GRANTED CANADIAN PATENT FOR SMART CARD PERSONALIZATION.
- NEXT YEAR'S BLACKBERRIES WILL BE NFC-EQUIPPED.
- SASKATOON TO LAUNCH CONTACTLESS TRANSIT SYSTEM.
- SCOTIABANK & RBC FIRST TO PUT INTERAC FLASH IN CUSTOMERS' WALLETS.
- TORONTO'S SMART CARD (TRANSIT) SYSTEM GOES LIVE.
- TTC MAY OPT FOR 'OPEN' ELECTRONIC FARE PAYMENT SYSTEM.
- VISA LAUNCHES FIRST DEBIT PRODUCT IN CANADA.
- VISA PAYWAVE TO PUMP UP SPEED & CONVENIENCE AT PETRO-CANADA LOCATIONS.
- ZOOMPASS ENHANCES MOBILE WALLET AND MAKES MONEY TRANSFERS FREE.

2009 Key highlights...

- Through 4 member-initiated Strategic Leadership teams and other services, ACT Canada helped members focus on:
  - government, identity management, merchant and mobile issues and opportunities
  - market issues and opportunities

Metrics

- 15 member events / workgroups
- 25 publications / reports / papers
- 7 speeches / briefings
- 2 government appointment / consultations / key interactions

The market...

- Most of the key industry stakeholders are involved in some form of emerging payment initiative
- Government of Canada introduces proposed Code of Conduct for Canadian Credit and Debit Card Industry
- Canada surpasses the 10+ million chip credit and debit cards in the Canadian market, with more rolling out daily to meet EMV liability shift
- Cardholders can now change EMV pins anywhere, anytime
- Enhanced Driver's licences (RFID) are issued and recalled by various province
- Multi-Lateral Steering Committee prepares Chip and PIN trial for Kitchener-Waterloo
- Merchants start to accept Chip and PIN
- Cross border fraud becomes a bigger issue
- Contactless use sees growth
- Telecomm moves mobile payment forward via Zoompass
- For NFC, mobile payment, EMV and other smart payment opportunities it is the business case, not technology that is the challenge.
- Montreal, Vancouver, Ottawa and GTA are all in the planning or roll out stages for smart fare cards
- E-passports are in trial with diplomatic corps

Board of Directors

Richard Adamson	Coinamatic Canada Inc.
Nino Di Teodoro	Citi Cards Canada Inc.
Sharon Fisk	ATB Financial
Catherine Johnston	ACT Canada
Sharon MacAlpine	HSBC Credit Card Services
Didier Serra	INSIDE Contactless
Allen Wright	Interac Association
Paul Zatychec	EWA-Canada Ltd

ACT Canada notes of interest

- ACT Canada launches our new look web site
- Former ACT Canada director is named new ombudsman for banking services and investments.

2009

Bringing members together and building an informed market

ACT Canada Member Events, Teams and Workgroups	Publications, Reports, Papers & Media	Speeches, Briefings
<ul><li>Annual Awards Celebration</li><li>Annual General Meeting</li><li>Cardware 09: Identity Management Insights conference for government (Ottawa)</li><li>Cardware 09: Payment Insights - Growth opportunities in troubling times (Toronto)</li><li>Cardware Connections Networking – Mobile Considerations (Oct)</li><li>Cardware Connections Networking – State of the Art Fraud Management and Mobile Opportunities (Mar)</li><li>Cardware Connections Networking – The Canadian Market (Feb, members only)</li><li>Government Strategic Leadership team</li><li>Identity Management Strategic Leadership team</li><li>Merchant Strategic Leadership team</li><li>Mobile Strategic Leadership team launched</li><li>PIN Management Strategic Leadership team</li><li>President's Advisory Council</li><li>Women In the Financial Sector Networking Evening</li><li>Women's Networking Committee</li></ul>	<ul><li>ACT news - driving insights (11 editions)</li><li>*Best EMV practices*</li><li>*Best practices for EMV implementation by merchants*</li><li>*Canada: Securing Payment* SmartCard International Journal</li><li>E-government.ca is launched</li><li>Euromonitor</li><li>IT Business</li><li>*Members Directory*</li><li>*Merchant Engagement* report</li><li>*Payment Card Industry review*</li><li>Payments Business Canada</li><li>*The Canadian payments market* Bloomberg interview</li><li>*The state of EMV in Canada* Cardworld</li><li>*The State of Identity Management in Canada*</li><li>*The state of identity management in Canada* networldwork.com</li></ul>	<ul><li>*Canadian Market Update*</li><li>Cardware 09: Identity Management Insights conference for government</li><li>*EMV: Canada and the United States* Smart Card Alliance -</li><li>*Growth opportunities in troubling times* Cardware 09: Payment Insights</li><li>RFID Forum breakfast briefing</li><li>*The Canadian Market* Cardware Connections Networking</li><li>*The Evolving Canadian Payments Landscape* Canadian Automatic Merchandising Association (CAMA) (Hamilton)</li></ul>

Key Additional Member Services	External Events (other)	Government Appointments, Interactions and Consultations
<ul><li>Department of Foreign and International Trade came to us several times looking for Canadian or non-Canadian members who could provide products or services</li><li>PIN Management Project Retail Merchant Association (Ontario) outreach</li><li>Review of merchant card flow process</li><li>Review of proposed card handling process for Cdn merchant</li><li>Royal Canadian Mint consulting services</li></ul>	<ul><li>Canadian Payments Association event – Toronto</li><li>Card conference – London UK</li><li>Cartes - Sesames Judge + ISCAN</li><li>Conference Board Security Council meeting – Ottawa</li><li>RFID Forum breakfast</li><li>Security Council Meeting (Ottawa)</li><li>Smart Card Alliance – Salt Lake City</li><li>Smart Card Alliance (New Orleans)</li><li>Smart Cards in Government (Washington)</li><li>University of Toronto privacy consultation roundtable</li></ul>	<ul><li>Catherine Johnston named Chair of the Canadian Advisory Committee (CAC) on CAC/ISO/IEC/JTC1/SC17 2006 – 2009</li><li>French Trade Delegation</li></ul>

and in the...

- ALMOST ALL CANADIANS USE LOYALTY PROGRAMMES.
- CANADA SURPASSES THE 10+ MILLION CHIP CREDIT AND DEBIT CARDS IN THE CANADIAN MARKET, WITH MORE ROLLING OUT DAILY TO MEET EMV LIABILITY SHIFT.
- CANADIAN TIRE DEPLOYS POSTILION SOLUTION TO ENABLE EMV CHIP PROGRAM.
- CANADIAN TIRE ROLLS OUT CHIP CARD TECHNOLOGY.
- CANADIAN TIRE TO INTRODUCE PREPAID MASTERCARD.
- CANADIAN TRANSIT AGENCY TO TEST SMART CARDS.
- CARDHOLDERS CAN NOW CHANGE EMV PINS ANYWHERE, ANYTIME.
- CHASE PAYMENTECH SIMPLIFIES CHIP AND PIN MIGRATION FOR INTEGRATED MERCHANTS.
- CONSULTATION ON PROPOSED CHANGES TO CPA RULE E1.
- FORMER ACT CANADA DIRECTOR NAMED NEW OMBUDSMAN FOR BANKING SERVICES AND INVESTMENTS.
- GIESECKE & DEVRIENT DELIVERS HIGH SECURITY RFID ENHANCED BORDER CROSSING CARDS.
- GOVERNMENT OF CANADA INTRODUCES PROPOSED CODE OF CONDUCT FOR CANADIAN CREDIT AND DEBIT CARD INDUSTRY.
- INTERAC AND CHINA UNIONPAY COLLABORATE TO PROVIDE CHINESE TRAVELLERS ACCESS TO CANADIAN ABMS.
- INTERAC PARTNERS WITH GLOBAL LEADER INSIDE TO BRING CONTACTLESS DEBIT TO CANADA.
- INTERAC QUALIFIES CONTACTLESS PAYMENT CERTIFICATION TEST PACKAGES FROM ICC SOLUTIONS.

- MASTERCARD CANADA BRINGS PAYPASS(TM) PAYMENTS TO BLACKBERRY SMARTPHONES.
- MASTERCARD CANADA, CITI CARDS CANADA & BELL MOBILITY COMPLETE MOBILE PAYMENT TRIAL.
- MCDONALD'S BEEFS UP SMART CARDS.
- OBERTHUR TECHNOLOGIES TO PROVIDE CONTACTLESS TRANSIT CARDS FOR MONTREAL'S PUBLIC TRANSPORT SYSTEM.
- ONE IN FOUR IS A VICTIM OF CARD FRAUD.
- PRIVACY COMMISSIONER WANTS OFF SWITCH ON NEW ONTARIO DRIVER LICENSES.
- QUEBEC LAUNCHES ENHANCED DRIVER LICENSES.
- RIM ANNOUNCES NEW BLACKBERRY SMART CARD READER.
- SASKATCHEWAN CANCELS RFID LICENCES
- SCOTIABANK PARTNERS WITH M-COM TO BRING MOBILE BANKING TO CANADIANS.
- SUBWAY'S CANADA STORES GO CONTACTLESS.
- TOUGH IDENTITY THEFT LAW IS PASSED BY CANADIAN GOVERNMENT.
- VISA PAYWAVE ANNOUNCED FOR COUNTRY STYLE & BLENZ THE CANADIAN COFFEE COMPANY.
- VISA PAYWAVE MAKES SHOPPING AT M&M MEAT SHOPS EVEN MORE CONVENIENT.
- WESTJET SELECTS RBC AND MASTERCARD FOR NEW TRAVEL REWARDS CARD.
- 'YOU'LL FIND IT ALL' AT JEAN COUTU AND CHECK-OUT FASTER WITH VISA PAYWAVE.
- ZOOMPASS LAUNCHES MOBILE PAYMENT SERVICE.

Canadian news

2008 Key highlights...

- Through member initiated Strategic Leadership teams and other services, ACT Canada helped members focus on:
  - government and
  - market issues and opportunities

Metrics

- 14 member events / workgroups
- 20 publications / reports / papers
- 11 speeches
- 5 government consultations / appointments

The market...

- Market focus shifts from technology to business opportunities
- The Competition Commissioner formally announces that the Competition Bureau will no longer oppose duality of membership in credit card networks that operate in Canada. This opened the door for financial institutions to offer credit cards from multiple card brands.
- Canada chip card trial sees success at midpoint.
- Contactless credit cards continue to move into the market
- Pin-less debits: proposed clearing framework announced by CPA.
- New report predicts 25 million will pay by mobile phone in 2011.
- Ontario gives city $7 million for transit smart cards.
- Canada ranks number one worldwide in online banking adoption, according to a survey of 37 countries

Board of Directors

Richard Adamson	Coinamatic Canada Inc.
Nino Di Teodoro	Citi Cards Canada Inc.
Sharon Fisk	ATB Financial
Catherine Johnston	ACT Canada
Sharon MacAlpine	HSBC Credit Card Services
Didier Serra	INSIDE Contactless
Allen Wright	Interac Association
Paul Zatychec	EWA-Canada Ltd

ACT Canada notes of interest

- ACT Canada becomes known as the stakeholder association, moving away from a technology focus and towards stakeholders
- ACT Canada joins the ITAC RFID Forum
- The Information Technology Association of Canada (ITAC) and ACT Canada share concerns expressed by Canada's Privacy Commissioners and Privacy Oversight Officials in their resolution titled Privacy Concerns about Enhanced Driver's Licences (February 5, 2008).
- Webinar education sessions launched

2008

Bringing members together and building an informed market

ACT Canada Member Events, Teams and Workgroups	Publications, Reports, Papers & Media	Speeches, Briefings
- Annual Awards - Annual General Meeting - Cardware 08: Managing identity in an interconnected world (Ottawa) - Cardware 08: Securing Payments (KW) - Cardware Connections - Vancouver - Cardware Connections Networking September - Cardware Connections Networking: Merchants and FI's - Education day - EMV Merchant Forums (2) to determine how they are proceeding, identify gaps in information or support that might be hampering their progress and to establish a new channel for them to access help - Government Strategic Leadership team - Merchants Strategic Leadership team - President's Advisory Council - Women in Payment networking meeting	- ACT news - driving insights (11 editions) - *Canada's migration to chip – for merchants* - *Cyber Security: Your Identity (Where your questions are more important than another's answers)* - Digital Exec magazine - *Members Directory* - *Mobile Payment Opportunities in Canada Research Report –* with IDC - *Canada: Another year of market growth* SCTI journal - Summit Magazine - *Worldwide e-ID initiatives* - www.emvcanada.ca is launched to provide information to stakeholders, consumers and media	- *A day in the Life...*ATB - *Canada, Identity and Privacy* CTST - Cardware 08: Securing Payments - *e-business: is it a dream or a plan?* University of Ottawa - e-commerce 2008 - *e-Payments* Royal Canadian Mint - *Managing ID in an interconnected world – Privacy Issues and Opportunities* - *Market briefing* Canada Post - *Market briefing* Lang Michener - *Online Identity Fraud* Lang Michener Law - *Online Identity Fraud: Part of a Greater Crime* Internet Law - Online Identity Theft (Toronto) - *The bad business of standards* ISAAC (ICT Standards Advisory Council of Canada)

Key Additional Member Services	External Events (other)	Government Appointments, Interactions and Consultations
<ul><li>ACT Canada joins the ITAC RFID forum</li><li>ATBureau - A day in the life…</li><li>Canada Post market briefing</li><li>Canadian Payments Association – Pinless Debit discussions</li><li>Clinic Card support</li><li>Member's Customer Day support and presentation</li><li>Mobile Payment Opportunities in Canada - members receive a $5k discount on the IDC study: Profiting from Mobile Payments.</li><li>Royal Canadian Mint Board - e-volution of the payments landscape</li><li>Royal Canadian Mint consulting services</li></ul>	<ul><li>Cartes - Sesames judge + ISCAN meeting</li><li>CTST</li><li>ITAC RFID workgroup, Vice-Chair</li><li>Multos anniversary meetings London</li><li>Treasury Board, Passport Canada meetings Ottawa</li><li>Visa Canada's 3rd Annual Security Symposium</li></ul>	<ul><li>Bank of Canada, Department of Foreign Affairs, Treasury Board, Passport Canada, FINTRAC</li><li>Canadian Payments Association - Stakeholders Advisory Council, Vice Chair</li><li>ISAAC: the Bad Business of Standards – Ottawa</li><li>Ontario Ministry of Government Services re impact of secure payment cards on health cards</li><li>Privacy Commissioners (provincial and federal) in Canada to raise awareness of the technological issues of enhanced drivers' licences in regards to privacy</li></ul>

and in the...

- CANADA CHIP CARD TRIAL SEEING SUCCESS AT MIDPOINT.
- CANADIAN AIRPORT WORKER ID CARD AWARDED.
- CANADIAN BROKERAGE ROLLS OUT BIOMETRIC VOICE AUTHENTICATION.
- CANADIAN CHIP CARD MARKET TRIAL A SUCCESS.
- CANADIAN E-PASSPORTS TO BE ISSUED IN 2011.
- CANADIAN PROVINCE REQUIRES ID THEFT ALERT OPTION. .
- CANADIAN TIRE MONEY GOES CONTACTLESS.
- CANADIANS FIRST IN ONLINE BANK USAGE NEW REPORT SAYS.
- CAPITAL ONE OFFERS PAYPASS CONTACTLESS TECHNOLOGY.
- CHASE PAYMENTECH PARTNERS WITH NBS PAYMENT SOLUTIONS TO OFFER A SUITE OF CHIP-AND-PIN TERMINALS.
- CIBC LAUNCHES NEW CHIP CARD TECHNOLOGY.
- EWA-CANADA SECURITY CONTENT AUTOMATION PROTOCOL (SCAP) TEST LAB ACCREDITATION AWARDED BY NIST & NVLAP.
- GEMALTO WEB SERVICE ENABLES PERSONALIZED PHOTOS ON PLASTICNOW MASTERCARD CARDS IN CANADA.
- ICC SOLUTIONS ANNOUNCES AVAILABILITY OF CANADIAN ACQUIRER TEST SOLUTIONS.
- INGENICO ANNOUNCES CLASS A CERTIFICATION FROM CHASE PAYMENTECH SOLUTIONS FOR ITS NEW TERMINALS.
- INTERAC CHIP TRANSITION GOES NATIONAL
- MARKET FOCUS SHIFTS FROM TECHNOLOGY TO BUSINESS OPPORTUNITIES
- MASTERCARD CANADA TRIALS MOBILE PAYMENT.
- MASTERCARD, CITI CARDS, BELL MOBILITY TRIAL MOBILE PAYMENTS.
- MONERIS BUYS KEYCORP CANADA.

- MONERIS TO PERFORM MERCHANT CERTIFICATION IN CANADA USING ICCSIM TEST SOLUTIONS.
- MONITISE & EVERLINK LAUNCH CANADIAN MOBILE PAYMENTS SERVICE.
- NATIONAL BANK OF CANADA COMPLETES SMART CARD TRANSACTIONS.
- NATIONAL BANK OF CANADA TO OFFER PAYPASS.
- NEW PRESIDENT APPOINTED TO GIESECKE & DEVRIENT CANADA.
- NEW REPORT PREDICTS 25 MILLION WILL PAY BY MOBILE PHONE IN 2011.
- ONTARIO GIVES CITY $7 MILLION FOR TRANSIT SMART CARDS.
- OTTAWA TO BENEFIT FROM CONTACTLESS FOR TRANSIT.
- PIN-LESS DEBITS: PROPOSED CLEARING FRAMEWORK ANNOUNCED BY CPA.
- RBC & VISA PREPARE TO JUMP MOBILE PAYMENT HURDLES.
- SMART CARDS COME TO MONTREAL TRANSIT. .
- TD VISA & TD MERCHANT SERVICES COMPLETE CANADA'S FIRST VISA PAYWAVE TRANSACTION.

Canadian news

- THE COMPETITION COMMISSIONER HAS FORMALLY ANNOUNCED THAT THE COMPETITION BUREAU WILL NO LONGER OPPOSE DUALITY OF MEMBERSHIP IN CREDIT CARD NETWORKS THAT OPERATE IN CANADA.
- TIM WILSON NAMED AS HEAD OF VISA CANADA.
- VANCOUVER MAY GET SMART CARD TRANSIT PROGRAM, BUT NOT UNTIL 2011.
- VISA PAYWAVE COMING TO TD VISA CARDS; TD MERCHANT SERVICES TO DEPLOY VISA PAYWAVE READERS.

2007 Key highlights...

- Through 3 member-initiated Strategic Leadership teams, 4 Cardware Connections, 2 conferences and other services, ACT Canada helped members focus on:
  - emerging markets and technologies
  - the financial sector and
  - merchant issues and opportunities
  - market issues and opportunities

Metrics

- 15 member events / workgroups
- 22 publications / reports / papers
- 14 speeches / briefings
- 6 government consultations / appointments

The market...

- Canadian payments industry commences chip trial in Kitchener-Waterloo, Ontario
- The payment market focuses on the chip trial although not all stakeholders have started preparations
- Canada is developing new EFT, E-Banking guidelines
- A surprising number of Canadians have knowledge of chip cards and opinions on security, convenience and even pricing according to an Ipsos Reid, ACT Canada study.
- Canadian government plans ID Theft Bill
- Canadians far exceed US consumers in loyalty activity
- Toronto to use contactless public transit ticketing
- 2 Canadian banks introduce mobile payment trials
- 1st debit transaction on chip at POS
- Both Tim Horton's and McDonald's start to accept contactless card transactions

ACT Canada notes of interest

- "Chip Cards in Canada: 2006" a syndicated consumer research study by IPSOS Reid and ACT Canada is released.
- Launches emvcanada.com to provide a forum for merchants, consumers and others to get EMV questions answered
- Releases new privacy design tools in response to governments and other issuers who choose to use contactless or RFID card technologies.
- The world is watching Canada and we are invited to speak at conferences around the world
- Members ask for new services ranging from training, to working with stakeholder groups such as merchants and consumers, to providing insights on market challenges and opportunities

2007

Bringing members together and building an informed market

ACT Canada Member Events, Teams and Workgroups	Publications, Reports, Papers & Media	Speeches, Briefings
- Annual General Meeting - Awards - Cardware 2007: EMV insights (Toronto) - Cardware Connections Networking - Market update - Cardware Connections Networking: Merchants and FI's - Cardware Connections: Chip Challenge - Cardware Connections: Fraud - Cardware: Identity Management & Credentialing Insights (Ottawa) - Emerging Markets and Technologies Strategic Leadership team launched - EMV training - Financial & Merchant Strategic Leadership team launched - Fraud and Chip Seminar - Merchant Committee - Merchant Workshop - President's Advisory Council	- ACT launches www.emvcanada.ca for merchants, consumers and the media - ACT news - driving insights (11 editions) - *Canada: a year of market growth* SCTI journal - *Contactless Smart Card Applications: Design Tool and Privacy Impact Assessment* - with the Information and Privacy Commissioner Ontario - *Identity Theft and Fraud in Healthcare: Pathology, Portents and Protection* (contributor) - IPSOS Reid -*Chip Cards in Canada* (Consumer Study) - *Members Directory* - *Merchant EMV faq's* - *Merchant Guidelines for PIN transactions* - Western Hemisphere Travel Initiative response to call for comments - *Will Canada push EMV into the US?* SecurID news interview - www.emvcanada.com is launched and features an interactive Q&A	- ACT Canada speaks at conferences in London, Nice, Beijing, Calgary and Banff - ATB Fraud presentation - *Canadians and Chip* Canadian Payments Association (Calgary) - CAN-ID - U of Ottawa Law Faculty - *Chip: how it will affect credit unions and your members* MACU - (Banff) - *EMV in Canada panel moderator* CTST - *EMV insights* Cardware 2007 - *ID Theft* Congress of Jewish Women - *Identity Management & Credentialing Insights* Cardware - Ombudsman Banking Services and Investments briefing - *Presentations on EMV, Canada's e-passport and host's opening remarks* World's First IC Summit (Beijing) - *Privacy and Security* E-Smart (Nice) - *Privacy and security: finding the balance* e-idWorld (London) - *Privacy by Design* Cardware Ottawa - *Privacy by design* Conference Board: Stronger Borders, Better Trade

Key Additional Member Services	External Events (other)	Government Appointments & Key Consultations
- ATB Fraud workshop presentation - Carta Business Plan development - OBSI briefing	- Cartes – Sesames Awards judge + ISCAN meeting - CTST – San Francisco - E-Smart – France - ETA - Las Vegas - Loyalty World conference & meetings with retailers (London) - Alliance Annual Conference - Government Technology (GTEC) – Ottawa - CPA Industry Forum on e-payments - Visa Security Symposium - Smart Card Alliance conference (Boston) - Visa Canada Security Symposium	- Chair of the Canadian Advisory Committee (CAC) on CAC/ISO/IEC/JTC1/SC17 - Canadian Payments Association - Stakeholders Advisory Council, Vice Chair - Government of Canada briefing on marketplace status - Ontario Government – smart cards for secure computer access - Proposals to improve the CPA Stakeholders Advisory Council - Smart Systems for Health briefing

and in the...

- "CHIP CARDS IN CANADA: 2006" A SYNDICATED CONSUMER RESEARCH STUDY BY IPSOS REID AND ACT CANADA IS RELEASED.
- ACT CANADA LAUNCHES EMVCANADA.COM TO PROVIDE A FORUM FOR MERCHANTS, CONSUMERS AND OTHERS TO GET EMV QUESTIONS ANSWERED
- ACT CANADA RELEASES NEW PRIVACY DESIGN TOOLS IN RESPONSE TO GOVERNMENTS AND OTHER ISSUERS WHO CHOOSE TO USE CONTACTLESS OR RFID CARD TECHNOLOGIES.
- BMO ADDS 'TAP & GO' CONVENIENCE TO MOSAIK MASTERCARD
- CANADA DEVELOPING NEW EFT, E-BANKING GUIDELINES
- CANADIAN BANK CUSTOMERS MOSTLY GO FOR CONVENIENCE SAYS REPORT
- CANADIAN GOVERNMENT PLANS ID THEFT BILL
- CANADIAN PAYMENTS INDUSTRY COMMENCES CHIP TRIAL IN KITCHENER-WATERLOO, ONTARIO
- CANADIAN TIRE PARTICIPATES IN INDUSTRY CHIP CARD PILOT
- CANADIANS FAR EXCEED US CONSUMERS IN LOYALTY ACTIVITY
- CHASE PAYMENTECH BECOMES 1ST CANADIAN ACQUIRER APPROVED BY MASTERCARD TO PROCESS CHIP TRANSACTIONS
- DESJARDINS SMART CARD TO BE LAUNCHED IN ST-JÉRÔME

- FIRST MASTERCARD CHIP TRANSACTION SIGNALS READINESS FOR ROLL-OUT ACROSS CANADA
- GEMALTO PUTS CANADIAN FINANCIAL INSTITUTIONS ON THE FAST TRACK TO SMART BANK CARDS
- GEMALTO WAS 1ST TO ACHIEVE INTERAC CERTIFICATION FOR SECURE BANKING IN CANADA
- GIESECKE & DEVRIENT SELECTED TO DELIVER ONTARIO'S NEW HIGH SECURITY DRIVER'S LICENCE

Canadian news

2006 Key highlights...

▪ Through 3 member initiated Strategic Leadership teams and other services, ACT Canada helped members focus on:
- ❑ opportunities to work with governments on card projects
- ❑ consumer reactions to chip
- ❑ stakeholders' roles and needs related to EMV
- ❑ market issues and opportunities

Metrics

- ❑ 13 member events / workgroups
- ❑ 30 publications / reports / papers
- ❑ 12 speeches / briefings
- ❑ 14 government consultations / appointments, key interactions

The market...

- ❑ The Canadian payment industry comes together to ensure a smooth migration to chip
- ❑ Members of the Canadian payment industry announce the chip technology trial
- ❑ The first chip debit transaction is expected to happen early 2007
- ❑ Most Canadians will have chip and pin cards by 2010
- ❑ GO (gov't of Ontario) charges ahead toward smart cards and outlines strategies for growth
- ❑ 2006 is certainly off and running with EMV conversion progressing in the financial services sector and much discussion of a cross border identification card in the public sector
- ❑ Toronto explores registered traveler card
- ❑ Transit smart card closer to reality - GTA multi-city project to start in mid-2007
- ❑ Prepaid cards gain in popularity

Board of Directors

Richard Adamson	Coinamatic Canada Inc.
Michele Davies	IBM Canada Ltd
Craig Diffie	Axalto
David Grindal	ACI
Catherine Johnston	ACT Canada
Allen Wright	Visa Canada Association
Paul Zatychec	EWA-Canada Ltd

ACT Canada notes of interest

- ACT Canada, along with Integrated Mobility Systems and Moving the Economy prepare a report on the Development of Innovative Smart Card Solutions for Canada.
- ACT Canada and Ipsos Reid are very pleased to announce the go-ahead for the "chip cards in Canada: 2006 " market research.
- The United Nations invites us to a roundtable discussion to discuss the needs of the United Nations and the capabilities of our members.
- Canada is the country of honour at Cartes, with special benefits and recognition for ACT Canada members

2006

Bringing members together and building an informed market

ACT Canada Member Events, Teams and Workgroups	Publications, Reports, Papers & Media	Speeches
<ul><li>Annual General Meeting</li><li>Awards</li><li>Cardware 06: EMV Optimization (Toronto)</li><li>Cardware 06: Identity is Everything - Made In Canada ID options and solutions (Ottawa)</li><li>Emerging Technologies, Applications and Markets Thought Leadership Council (TLC)</li><li>Financial Services Strategic Leadership Team</li><li>Government Strategic Leadership team</li><li>Integrated Mobility Solutions Symposium</li><li>Moving the Economy Symposium</li><li>President's Advisory Council</li><li>Smart Cards 101 – 2006 training</li><li>Stakeholders Strategic Leadership team</li><li>Web education</li></ul>	<ul><li>*"Business Relationships between the Financial Sector and Transit / Transportation Initiatives"*</li><li>ACT news - driving insights (11 editions)</li><li>*Canada in the global market* Cartes interview:</li><li>*Canada: a market on the move* Cards Asia</li><li>*Canada: cards on the move* SCTI Journal</li><li>*Development of Innovative Smart Card Solutions for Canada*</li><li>*EMV benefits* Card Technology Magazine</li><li>*EMV whitepaper*</li><li>*Glossary of Terms – Version 4*</li><li>*Identifying Barriers to Financial Sector Partnerships Research report*</li><li>*Identity Fraud* Vice Squad TV</li><li>*Identity is everything* Summit Magazine</li><li>*Identity Theft and the Criminal Code submission* Department of Justice (Cda)</li><li>*Identity Theft Tip Sheet*</li><li>*Members Directory*</li><li>*Privacy and Security: Balancing Our Best Interests*</li><li>*Smart Card Technology Glossary of Terms 2006*</li><li>*Transit fraud* Toronto Sun interview</li><li>Web site – added content and redesign</li><li>*What CEOs need to know about Smart Card technology*</li></ul>	<ul><li>*EMV Optimization* Cardware 06</li><li>*Identity Fraud* Risk Management Association</li><li>*Identity is Everything - Made In Canada ID options and solutions* Cardware 06</li><li>*Identity theft and information security in healthcare - Information at Risk* Sunnybrook ID in Healthcare:</li><li>Integrated Mobility Solutions Symposium</li><li>Moving the Economy Symposium</li><li>*Secure identification and the use of advanced card technologies by government* Conference Board of Canada: Public-private sector national security summit</li><li>Smart Card 101 workshops (3) - instructor</li><li>*Smart Moves in Canada* for D&H</li><li>*Transit and transportation opportunities involving payment cards* Transport Canada</li></ul>

Key Additional Member Services	External Events (other)
<ul><li>Funding assistance procured for SMEs to attend foreign conferences and arranged discounts for others</li><li>Trade trip to Cartes for members</li></ul>	<ul><li>Cartes - Canada is the country of honour</li><li>Visa Security Symposium</li><li>E-Smart Conference</li></ul>

Government Appointments	Government Key Consultations	Government Key Interactions
<ul><li>Appointed to the U of T IPSI Advisory Board of CAN ID? Visions for Canada: Identity Policy Projections and Policy Alternatives</li><li>Canadian Advisory Committee (CAC) on CAC/ISO/IEC/JTC1/SC17 2006 - 2009 - appointed Chair</li><li>Canadian Payments Association - Stakeholders Advisory Council, vice chair</li></ul>	<ul><li>Department of Justice (Cda) - "IDENTITY THEFT: Consultation On Proposals to Amend The Criminal Code" consultation (2 consultations)</li><li>Royal Canadian Mint briefing</li><li>Transport Canada - "Business Relationships between the Financial Sector and Transit / Transportation Initiatives" for the Technical Specifications for the Development of Innovative Smart Card Solutions for Canadian Transit</li><li>Comments on proposed changes to the CPA E1 rule, Exchange of Shared Electronic Point-of-Service Payment Items for the Purpose of Clearing and Settlement to Accommodate Chip Technology</li></ul>	<ul><li>Australian task force studying consumer and privacy issues relevant to the implementation of the new Australian Access Card system</li><li>Ontario Ministry of Health, Government Services and Australia delegation re health card fraud</li><li>Secure identification and the use of advanced card technologies by governments – presentation</li><li>United Nations – invited by the Government of Canada to participate at Roundtable discussions between UN procurement officials and Canadian information communications technology experts</li><li>UK municipal government delegation looking for a Canadian municipality to participate in a citizen's services project.</li><li>US Consulate</li></ul>

- 12 CANADIAN ISSUERS & 5 ACQUIRERS COMMIT TO INTRODUCE MASTERCARD CHIP CARDS
- 20,000+ CANADIAN MERCHANT LOCATIONS PARTICIPATING IN MASTERCARD QUICK PAYMENT SERVICE PROGRAM
- 2006 IS CERTAINLY OFF AND RUNNING WITH EMV CONVERSION PROGRESSING IN THE FINANCIAL SERVICES SECTOR AND MUCH DISCUSSION OF A CROSS BORDER IDENTIFICATION CARD IN THE PUBLIC SECTOR.
- 2200+ CANADIAN INTERNET MERCHANTS JOIN MASTERCARD SECURECODE PROGRAM
- ACT CANADA AND IPSOS REID ARE VERY PLEASED TO ANNOUNCE THE GO-AHEAD FOR THE "CHIP CARDS IN CANADA: 2006 " MARKET RESEARCH.
- ACT CANADA, ALONG WITH INTEGRATED MOBILITY SYSTEMS AND MOVING THE ECONOMY PREPARE A REPORT ON THE DEVELOPMENT OF INNOVATIVE SMART CARD SOLUTIONS FOR CANADA.
- CANADIAN FIRST: FIRST NATIONS TO RECEIVE SOCIAL ASSISTANCE BENEFITS ON PREPAID CARDS
- COLLIS APPROVED AS INTERAC TEST TOOL VENDOR
- CUETS & EVERLINK ANNOUNCE ALLIANCE TO PROVIDE CHIP SOLUTIONS TO CREDIT UNIONS AND CAISSES POPULAIRES
- CUETS TEAMS WITH BELL ID & ACONITE FOR SWITCH TO EMV
- EDMONTON TRANSIT BETS ON 'SMART' CARDS
- FIVE LEADING PAYMENT BRANDS UNITE TO STRENGTHEN GLOBAL DATA SECURITY
- GEMALTO FIRST TO ACHIEVE NEW SECURITY LEVELS PROTECTING CANADIAN BANKCARD HOLDERS FROM IDENTITY THEFT
- GIESECKE & DEVRIENT OPENS STATE-OF-THE-ART SMART CARD FACILITY IN CANADA
- GO (GOV'T OF ONTARIO) CHARGES AHEAD TOWARD SMART CARDS AND OUTLINES STRATEGIES FOR GROWTH
- ICC SOLUTIONS ASSISTS WITH DEVELOPMENT OF REQUIREMENTS FOR INTERAC TEST TOOLS
- KEYCORP BUYS CANADIAN ETPOS FIRM
- MASTERCARD'S PAYPASS MOVES INTO CINEPLEX ENTERTAINMENT THEATERS
- MEMBERS OF THE CANADIAN PAYMENT INDUSTRY ANNOUNCE THE CHIP TECHNOLOGY TRIAL
- MINT & NOW PREPAY GO LIVE WITH THE 1ST NATIONWIDE RETAIL NETWORK DESIGNED FOR RELOADING PREPAID CREDIT CARDS IN CANADA
- RBC CONTRACTS ACI FOR CHIP MIGRATION
- TAP & GO AT RABBA FINE FOODS WITH MASTERCARD PAYPASS
- THE CANADIAN PAYMENT INDUSTRY COMES TOGETHER TO ENSURE A SMOOTH MIGRATION TO CHIP
- TORONTO EXPLORES REGISTERED TRAVELER CARD
- TRANSIT SMART CARD CLOSER TO REALITY - GTA MULTI-CITY PROJECT TO START IN MID-2007

Canadian news

2005 Key highlights...

- Through 4 member-initiated Thought Leadership teams and other services, ACT Canada helped members focus on:
    - emerging technologies and markets,
    - financial services,
    - government
    - retailer opportunities and issues
    - market issues and opportunities

Metrics

- 19 member events / workgroups
- 22 publications / reports / papers
- 13 speeches / briefings
- 11 government consultations / appointments, key interactions

The market...

- In 2005, Canada has moved from a potential market to an inevitable advanced card market with benefits for Canadians in terms of greater security and convenience in our day-to-day transactions.
- INTERAC Association announces its decision to move to chip
- Visa announces liability shift for fall 2010
- MasterCard International confirms that its chip solutions are ready for implementation in Canada
- Mississauga gives the official go-ahead to participating in the Greater Toronto Area's electronic smart card transit fare project.
- Study says it will take seven years for smart cards to make a dent in the U.S.
- Canada's major banks are finalizing details for a service that will allow consumers to use their debit cards to make purchases on the web
- The use of gift cards is growing so rapidly it's causing a shift in retail spending patterns, according to a study by Statistics Canada
- First prepaid Visa gift cards introduced in Canada
- RIM (Blackberry) announces the Blackberry Smart Card Reader
- Contactless enters payments discussions
- MasterCard and Visa Agree to a Common Contactless Communications Protocol

Board of Directors

Richard Adamson   Coinamatic
Douglas Beardshaw   DEVMARK
Sandra Bergen   CUETS
Geoffrey Bowen   Ingenico
Michele Davies   IBM Canada Ltd
Nagesh Devata   MasterCard Canada
Justin Fraser   Retail Logic
Ed Gresham   Giesecke & Devrient (G&D)
Catherine Johnston   ACT Canada
Gary McDonald   Canadian Passport Office
Miki Radovjsa   Airos Group
Pat Ranney   CIBC
Will Tam   Scotiabank

ACT Canada notes of interest

- ACT Canada establishes the EMV Stakeholders Office
- Members receive sweeping new benefits
- The President's Advisory Council is established
- Acquirers are given 26 questions about EMV to help them connect with other stakeholders

2005

Bringing members together and building an informed market

ACT Canada Member Events, Teams and Workgroups	Publications, Reports, Papers & Media	Speeches, Briefings
<ul><li>Annual General Meeting</li><li>Awards</li><li>Cardware 05: Smart Moves</li><li>Cardware Connections Networking – "Public Transit: Wherever Life Takes You"</li><li>Cardware Connections Networking – EMV – "the early bird gets the worm"</li><li>Emerging Technologies, Applications and Markets Strategic Leadership team</li><li>EMV Stakeholder Forum workshop for Government</li><li>EMV Stakeholder Management Forum</li><li>Financial Services Strategic Leadership team</li><li>Government Strategic Leadership team</li><li>IMS-MTE Briefing Session</li><li>National Card Advancement Committee launched</li><li>National Card Advancement research project</li><li>Networking event</li><li>President's Advisory Council</li><li>Retailer Stakeholder Strategic Leadership team launched</li><li>2nd annual closed briefing session on secure identification and the use of advanced card technologies by governments & private sector</li><li>Smart Card 101 training</li><li>UK retailers' EMV conversion experiences presentation</li></ul>	<ul><li>*31 Questions Retailers should ask about EMV conversion*</li><li>ACTion news (11 editions)</li><li>*Card Fraud Solutions* Canada AM</li><li>*Global Payment Market review*</li><li>*Glossary of Terms – Version 3*</li><li>*How smart card applications could increase sales* Canadian Professional Sales Association Magazine</li><li>*Members Directory*</li><li>*Privacy Impact Assessment for Contactless Cards* - with the IPC/O</li><li>*Q&A on the North American card market* Cards Asia</li><li>*Questions governments should ask about EMV and ID management*</li><li>*The Canadian Market in 2005: Emerging from a Vision to National Roll Outs* SCTI Journal</li><li>*Use of chip technology* Media Multicom</li></ul>	<ul><li>ACT Canada Smart Card Primer 2005 - instructor</li><li>*Authentication –The Next Generation panel moderator* Canadian Payments Association Panorama (St John's)</li><li>*Canadian market update* CardTech/SecurTech</li><li>Cardware 05: Smart Moves</li><li>*EMV Stakeholder Forum workshop* for Government</li><li>EMV Stakeholder Management Forum</li><li>IMS-MTE Briefing Session</li><li>*Prepaid Cards Report* Canadian Payments Association</li><li>Royal Canadian Mint Board of Directors - Cardware briefing</li><li>Second annual closed briefing session on secure identification and the use of advanced card technologies by governments and the private sector</li><li>Smart Card 101 training</li><li>*Smart Card Market update* for IBM</li><li>*The Chip Roadmap presentation* CUCC Chip Migration Task Force</li></ul>

Key Additional Member Services	External Events (other)
▪ CUCC Chip Migration Task Force - The Chip Roadmap presentation ▪ Smart Card Market update for IBM	▪ Cartes + ISCAN meeting ▪ ICMA ▪ Smart Card Alliance ▪ Public Policy Forum – Ottawa ▪ Retailer meetings in London UK

Government Appointments	Government Key Consultations	Government Key Interactions
▪ Canadian Payments Association - Stakeholders Advisory Council, Vice Chair	▪ Federal Government Briefings (hosted by Passport Canada) 17 agencies present ▪ IMS-MTE briefing ▪ Justice Canada consults ACT on potential changes to the Criminal Code to deal with identity theft ▪ Ontario government - Doing Business with the Ontario Government - oral and written submissions ▪ Public Works and Government Services Canada, Information Technology Services Branch - vendor outreach strategy consultation ▪ Royal Canadian Mint – smart card presentation	▪ 17 government groups meet with ACT Canada to discuss card plans ▪ Public Works and Government Services – Roundtable on ITSB Vendor Outreach Strategy ▪ RCMP ask for assistance in a payment fraud investigation ▪ Secure Identification and the use of advanced card technologies use by governments

and in the...

- 1ST PREPAID VISA GIFT CARDS INTRODUCED IN CANADA
- ACI READIES CANADIAN CUSTOMERS FOR INTERAC CHIP CARD MIGRATION
- AXALTO OPENS ADVANCED PAYMENT CARD PERSONALIZATION CENTER IN CANADA
- BURGER KING CANADA SPEEDS MASTERCARD PAYMENT
- CANADIAN MARKET STRATEGIC INITIATIVES
- CANADIAN TIRE TO INVEST IN MODERN POS SYSTEM
- CANADIANS ASK FOR FASTER & BETTER LOYALTY REWARDS
- CHIP CARDS PREDICTED TO REDUCE GLOBAL ATM FRAUD
- COINAMATIC SELECTS NEW HYPERCOM CREDIT/DEBIT CARD TERMINALS FOR INNOVATIVE SMARTCITY SMART CARD RELOAD SYSTEM
- CONTACTLESS CREDIT CARD TRANSACTIONS DISPLAYED AT CARDWARE SHOW
- CREDIT UNION MASTERCARD LEADING THE WAY TO CHIP
- DEBIT CARD SHOPPING COMING TO THE WEB
- DESJARDINS TO SWITCH TO CHIP TECHNOLOGY
- DEXIT CONFIRMS UK TRANSIT BID
- DEXIT OPENS IN OTTAWA
- G&D READY TO DELIVER THE SPEED AND FLEXIBILITY OF CONTACTLESS
- GEMPLUS TO DEVELOP R-UIM SMART CARDS FOR TELUS MOBILITY
- GIFT CARD STUDY CONFIRMS GROWING IMPACT
- INTERAC ASSOCIATION ANNOUNCES DECISION TO MOVE TO CHIP
- LASERCARD ANNOUNCES $8 MILLION FOLLOW-ON ORDER FOR CANADIAN PERMANENT RESIDENT CARDS
- MASTERCARD'S CHIP SOLUTIONS READY FOR IMPLEMENTATION IN CANADA

- MINT & PEOPLES TRUST PARTNER WITH IDTEL FINANCIAL
- MINT PARTNERS TO ESTABLISH A NATIONWIDE ROLLOUT FOR SALE & RELOADING OF PREPAID CREDIT CARDS
- MISSISSAUGA TO HOP ABOARD 'SMART' FARES
- MULTIPLE BENEFITS FOUND TO DRIVE EMV ADOPTION
- PAYMENT PROVIDER MONERIS SOLUTIONS PROCESSES CANADA'S FIRST INTERAC ONLINE TRANSACTION
- QI SYSTEMS DEVELOPING SMART-CARD ID & PAYMENT SYSTEM FOR OSAGE NATION

Canadian news

2004 Key highlights...

- Through 8 member initiated Thought Leadership teams and other services, ACT Canada helped members focus on:
  - emerging technologies and markets,
  - financial services,
  - government and retailer opportunities and issues
  - national infrastructure and card advancement
  - market issues and opportunities

Metrics

- 17 member events / workgroups
- 27 publications/reports/papers
- 14 speeches / briefings
- 11 government consultations / appointments, key interactions

The market...

- Smart cards move into the market and the technology is seen as no more than an appropriate platform to support a need or opportunity.
- EMV migration dates for Visa issuers are expected between 2007 and 2010
- The role of the internet for individual stakeholder groups becomes a focal point
- CATSA, the government transportation security initiative plans to issue smart cards with biometrics to staff at airports – 10 airports are in the pilot
- 90,000 Department of National Defense personnel carry a smart card to provide the key to an end-to-end, tamper-proof data and message handling system.
- The new optical Canadian Permanent Resident Card replaces paper ID, significantly raising the bar for counterfeit and tamper resistant identification.
- Other public sector initiatives include transit and hazardous waste tracking
- Private sector initiatives include worker credentialing, loyalty programs and security
- Scotiabank runs a multi-app pilot in Barrie

Board of Directors

Richard Adamson	Coinamatic
Douglas Beardshaw	DEVMARK Technology Management
Sandra Bergen	CUETS
Geoffrey Bowen	Ingenico
Bob Cheriton	Insight Navigation
Michele Davies	IBM Canada Ltd
Michael de Rosenroll	Treasury Board Secretariat of Canada
Craig Diffie	Axalto
Rebecca Dornbusch	International Biometrics Industry Association
Ed Gresham	Giesecke & Devrient:
David Grindal	ACI Worldwide (Canada) Inc.
Bryce Hutt	Scotiabank
Catherine Johnston	ACT Canada
Gary McDonald	Canadian Passport Office
Miki Radivojsa	Airos Group
Pat Ranney	CIBC
Randy Vanderhoof	Smart Card Alliance
Allen Wright	Visa Canada Association

ACT Canada notes of interest

- The association's vision is that advocacy and issues management will build market awareness and enthusiasm, leading to market confidence and adoption
- The members' only section of the web site is activated to give ACT Canada members access to privileged information
- President's Advisory Council is launched
- International Smart Card Associations Network (ISCAN) – ACT Canada becomes Chair
- National Issuers and Infrastructure Committee is launched to address the market's focus

2004

Bringing members together and building an informed market

ACT Canada Member Events, Teams and Workgroups	Publications, Reports, Papers & Media	Speeches, Briefings
▪ 1st Canadian Smart Card Summit and Golf Tournament ▪ Annual General Meeting ▪ Awards ▪ Cardware 04: Innovation and Your Bottom Line ▪ Closed Door Government Briefing - Ottawa ▪ Emerging Technologies Standards and Market Strategic Leadership team (SLT) ▪ E-Terrorism and protecting your customer's privacy ▪ Financial Services SLT ▪ Government SLT ▪ Government Stakeholder Forum launched ▪ National Card Advancement Committee launched ▪ National Issuers and Infrastructure ▪ Networking reception ▪ President's Advisory Council ▪ Retailer Stakeholder Forum ▪ Security Forum ▪ Stakeholder SLT	▪ ACTion news (11 editions) ▪ *Advanced Card Technology primer* ▪ *Canadian Payments Market review* ▪ *Card Facts* ▪ *Chip cards to increase retail sales* Contact Magazine ▪ *Chip technology for student cards* Canwest Media ▪ *ID Theft* Bankrate.com ▪ IDC research and Frost and Sullivan - biometrics ▪ *Identity Theft information sheet* ▪ *Market Update* ▪ *Members Directory* ▪ Retail Banking Research on current status and future plans for EMV migration worldwide, with a focus on countries such as Canada ▪ *Retailer Position Paper* (RSF) ▪ Smart Card International Journal article ▪ *Smart Card Technology Glossary of Terms 2004* ▪ *Testing and certification criteria for Multi-Application Privacy Impact Assessments* ▪ W5 interview	▪ *Canadian market update* ▪ Canadian Smart Card Summit ▪ *Card Technology panel moderator* Inside ID (Washington) ▪ Closed Door Government Briefing - Ottawa ▪ *e-commerce: is it the dot.com of the decade?* University of Ottawa E-commerce law workshop ▪ *E-Terrorism: protecting your customer's privacy* (with the Information Privacy Commissioner Ontario) ▪ *Government, e-government and EMV* ▪ *Identity theft* CPA SAC ▪ *Identity theft: you've been robbed* Canadian Payments Association ▪ Industry Canada & Transport Canada, Security and Technology – speaker ▪ *Innovation and Your Bottom Line* Cardware 04 ▪ *Privacy by Design* Industry Canada Security Technology Symposium (Ottawa) ▪ *Privacy Impact Assessment Procedure for Multi-App Smart Cards* (with the Information Privacy Commissioner Ontario) ▪ Smart card seminar instructor

Key Additional Member Services	External Events (other)
▪ Business Opportunity Bulletin (St John's)	▪ Cartes ▪ GOVSEC in Washington ▪ Smart Card Alliance – Government show ▪ CTST ▪ Security Technology Symposium

Government Appointments	Government Key Consultations	Government Key Interactions
▪ Canadian Payments Association - Stakeholders Advisory Council, Vice Chair	▪ Department of Justice (Cda) consults with ACT on options for reform to address issues pertaining to identity theft ▪ Federal Privacy Commissioner and Ontario Commissioner meeting to discuss market issues ▪ Government (CDA) briefing session attended by multiple ministries - hosted by Passport Canada ▪ IMS-MTE Briefing Session ▪ Public Works and Government Services Consultation ▪ Transport Canada & Industry Canada - Privacy by design	▪ Passport Canada - Advanced Card Technologies and Government presentation ▪ Privacy Commissioner's office meeting to discuss Common Criteria for Privacy Certification ▪ Ontario Ministry of Transportation ▪ Recommend 10 members to assist Public Works and Governments Services Canada in identifying ways to increase efficiency and effectiveness in the delivery of IT services and infrastructure to government departments and agencies.

and in the...

- CANADA PLANS SMART CARD ID FOR AIRPORT WORKERS
- CANADIAN BANK BUYS INGENICO SMART CARD TERMINALS
- CATSA PILOT PROJECT AWARDED
- CELL PHONES BECOME MOBILE PARKING METERS IN TORONTO
- CONTACTLESS PAYMENT PROVIDER LOOKS BEYOND CANADA
- CONTACTLESS SMART CARDS FLY WITH CATSA
- EASYPARK & MINT INTRODUCE 'PARK & PAY BY PHONE' SERVICE IN VANCOUVER
- E-PAYMENTS DRIVE ONE-QUARTER OF CANADA'S ECONOMIC GROWTH
- G&D IN CANADA TO DELIVER GROUND BREAKING SMART VISA CARD
- GO TRANSIT TAKES FIRST STEP TOWARD GTA SMART-CARD FARE SYSTEM; PROJECT MANAGER HIRED TO DEVISE PLAN
- HP CANADA TO DELIVER NEXT-GENERATION GREEN MACHINE AND POINT-OF-SALE CAPABILITIES
- ISCAN ELECTIONS - ACT CANADA BECOMES CHAIR
- KEYCORP IN WIRELESS PAYMENT SYSTEM FOR CANADIAN TAXIS
- MASTERCARD TO INTRODUCE PAYPASS IN CANADA
- OTTAWA TO ISSUE DIGITAL PASSPORT
- PAY@TABLE MARKET: NEW SOLUTION LAUNCHED IN CANADA
- SMART-CARD USE WISE FOR FUTURE, TTC DECIDES
- TORONTO PARKING AUTHORITY SELECTS MINT INC. FOR NEW TPA CORPORATE PARKING CARD

Canadian news

2003 Key highlights...

- Through 6 member-initiated teams and other services, ACT Canada helped members focus on:
  - Interoperability and Infrastructure whitepapers
  - Privacy Impact Assessment Procedure for Multi-application Smart Cards
  - building government business cases for smart cards
  - market issues and opportunities

Metrics

- 24 member events / workgroups
- 36+ publications/reports/papers
- 24 speeches / briefings
- 19 government consultations / appointments, key interactions

The market...

- Visa Canada announces their move to EMV
- The Government of Canada looks at the role of smart cards in identity management
- Identity theft is a rapidly growing issue
- RBC launches Canada's first national VISA chip card.

Board of Directors

Richard Adamson	Coinamatic
Bob Aylward	RBC Financial Grooup
Douglas Beardshaw	DEVMARK Technology Management
Sandra Bergen	CUETS
Geoffrey Bowen	Ingenico
Bob Cheriton	Insight Navigation
Michael de Rosenroll	Treasury Board Secretariat of Canada
Rebecca Dornbusch	International Biometrics Industry Association
Ed Gresham	Giesecke & Devrient:
David Grindal	ACI Worldwide (Canada) Inc.
Bryce Hutt	Scotiabank
Catherine Johnston	ACT Canada
Francois LeBel	SchlumbergerSema
Gary McDonald	Canadian Passport Office
Cindy Pearson	Smart Toronto
Randy Vanderhoof	Smart Card Alliance
Allen Wright	Visa Canada Association

ACT Canada notes of interest

- The association contributes to Retail Banking research
- 1st use of the ACT Canada/IPCO Privacy Impact Assessment Procedure for Multi-application Smart Cards
- ACT Canada initiates talks with CTST and the Smart Card Alliance to hold a North American wide conference

2003

Bringing members together and building an informed market

ACT Canada Member Events, Teams and Workgroups	Publications, Reports, Papers & Media	Speeches, Briefings
• 1st use of the ACT Canada/IPCO Privacy Impact Assessment Procedure for Multi-application Smart Cards – PIA Audit	• *2nd annual issues survey*	• Breaking through Card Barriers Conference
• 4 groups developing Interoperability and Infrastructure whitepapers for the Driving Solutions roundtable	• ACTion news (11 editions)	• *e-government and Smart Cards briefing*
• Annual General Meeting	• *An Assessment of Business Liability & Risk associated with the implementation of the Community of Interest (CoI) concept*	• *e-mobility and smart cards* Ajax Business Group
• Awards	• *Briefing Paper - Public Awareness of Card Fraud Issues*	• *e-mobility and smart cards* IMS-MTE New Mobility Forum
• Breaking through Card Barriers Conference - case studies	• Canadian Security magazine	• *EMV: an International Perspective* events (2)
• Building Government Business Cases workgroup	• Card Forum International article	• *Government - e-government and EMV*
• Education and Networking meetings	• *Chip cards: privacy enabling by design*	• *Identity Theft and Governments: Putting You At Risk* ID Smart - Smart Cards in Government and Health (London UK)
• e-government and Smart Cards briefing	• FutureZone tv and media interviews on *a national ID card, EMV announcement and identity theft*	• *Identity theft and governments: putting you at risk* Public Policy Forum on Identity theft and ID fraud
• EMV: an International Perspective events (Toronto and Ottawa)	• *Identity Fraud* Leading Edge	• *Identity Theft* Durham Business Connections
• Intellectual Property 101 Network Education Meeting	• *Identity fraud: are you a victim?* SCTI journal	• *Identity theft: you are at risk* 2nd Worldwide ID Congress
• Market Intelligence Roundtable - Driving Solutions	• *Identity Fraud: You are a victim!* Leading Edge Magazine	• *Identity theft: you are at risk* Canadian Payments Association conference
• MTE (Moving the Economy), in association with ACT Canada, two Cross-Industry Sessions	• Inside Card Technology Magazine	• *Identity theft: you are at risk* CTST
• National Issuer and Infrastructure Committee	• *Insurance industry briefing*	• Optical Card technology seminar - instructor
• Privacy Protection workgroup	• *Intellectual Property 101*	• *Privacy by Design*
• Retailer breakfast and Advanced Card 101 seminar	• *Issues Survey*	• *Privacy by Design: How to do a Privacy Impact Assessment for Multi-Application Smart Cards*
• Smart Card 2003 seminars	• *Members Directory*	• Smart Cards in Government (Arlington)
• Smart Card Technology Glossary of Terms 2003 workgroup	• Print and radio interviews re ISM and New York database hack	• Retailer breakfast and Advanced Card 101 seminar
• Smart World - written roundtable on identity cards, with APSCA and Smartex	• *Privacy impact assessment of the collection and distribution of multi-program data through a community-of-interest service delivery system*	• Smart Card 2003 seminars
• Solutions Roundtable event	• *Research report on more than 20 implementations and how they dealt with infrastructure, interoperability, security, standards, business case development and privacy*	• Smart Card Technology seminar - instructor
• Transit and transportation sector cross industry briefing	• Technology Magazine	• Smart Cards 101 (for PMAC members)

Publications, Reports, Papers & Media	Speeches, Briefings
- *Secure ID cards* Card - *Security Products and Services* article - *Smart Card Technology Glossary of Terms* 2003 - Smart World - written roundtable on identity cards, with APSCA and Smartex - *Steps to do a Privacy Impact Assessment for Multi-Application Smart Cards* - *The Canadian Market – It's not about the technology* SCTI journal - *The impact of advanced cards on merchants, travel and tourism* Luggage, Leathergoods and Accessories	- *Smart Cards in Government* Smart Card Alliance - Solutions Roundtable event - *The Canadian Market* Cartes - Transit and transportation sector cross industry briefing

Key Additional Member Services	External Events (other)
<ul><li>2nd Annual market survey</li><li>Business Opportunity bulletins</li><li>ISCAN updates on foreign market activities</li><li>Members saved $94,091 through complimentary passes and discounts to ACT events and an unknown amount through external offers</li><li>Negotiated discounts for members at external conferences and advertising and complimentary subscriptions</li><li>Privacy Protection Assessment</li><li>Visa Canada member Workshop</li><li>Worker Credentialing Management System – Privacy Impact Assessment</li></ul>	<ul><li>Cartes</li><li>IMS Cross 1st Industry briefing</li><li>Inside ID (Washington)</li><li>ISCAN meetings</li><li>Purchasing Management Association of Canada – joint education meetings</li><li>Retail Council of Canada - discussions</li><li>Smart Card Alliance – Government (Arlington VA)</li><li>Smart Cards for Government and Healthcare (London)</li><li>Smart Toronto launch</li><li>US Counsel General - discussions</li><li>Visa Canada member workshops</li></ul>

Government Appointments	Government Key Consultations	Government Key Interactions
<ul><li>Canadian Payments Association - Stakeholders Advisory Council, Vice Chair (3 year appointment by the Minister of Finance)</li></ul>	<ul><li>Citizenship and Immigration Forum and Privy Council on Biometrics: Implications and Applications for Citizenship and Immigration - policy discussions participant</li><li>Department of Citizenship and Immigration requested a briefing on the difference between optical and smart cards, and other information</li><li>Government of Canada – Architecture Review Board briefing</li><li>Government of Canada asks ACT Canada to develop a strategy paper</li><li>Ministry of Consumer and Corporate Service asks ACT Canada to review their PIA</li><li>Public Policy Forum: Roundtable Discussion on Identity Theft and Identity Fraud for the Standing Committee on Citizenship and Immigration</li><li>US Government (DOD) briefing on privacy assessments</li></ul>	<ul><li>Architecture Review Board (federal) - e-government and smart cards presentation</li><li>Architecture Review Board (Federal) – identity theft</li><li>e-government and Smart Cards briefing</li><li>Government of Ontario co-develops Business Liability and Risk Assessment procedure with ACT Canada</li><li>Honourable J Ecker – identity theft</li><li>Law enforcement</li><li>Passport Canada</li><li>Public Works and Governments Services Canada asks ACT Canada to recommend 10 members to comment on ways to increase efficiency and effectiveness in the delivery of IT services and infrastructure to government departments and agencies</li><li>Treasury Board</li><li>US Consulate</li><li>US Counsel General - discussions on synergies</li></ul>

and in the...

- ACI WORLDWIDE & HP CANADA HOST EMV SEMINAR IN SEPTEMBER
- AMENITY ONE™ LAUNCHES NEW CALE DEVICES WITH SMARTCITY® CARDS
- AMERICAN EXPRESS SELECTED TO PARTNER WITH AEROPLAN
- ATM SWIPE-&-SNAP SCAM NETTED $620,000, COURT TOLD
- BIOMETRICS ARE COMING TO CANADA, MINISTER SAYS
- CATA & SMART TORONTO TECHNOLOGY ALLIANCE MERGE
- CHIP-BASED PASSPORTS GAIN MOMENTUM
- CHRYSALIS-ITS & WEBPAY PROVIDE INTEGRATED SOLUTIONS TO HELP COMBAT ONLINE FRAUD
- COINAMATIC APPOINTED CANADIAN DISTRIBUTOR OF CALE PAY & DISPLAY PARKING DEVICES
- CPI READY TO SUPPORT VISA CANADA MEMBER INSTITUTIONS AS THEY MIGRATE
- CREDIT UNION CENTRAL OF CANADA SIGNS EXCLUSIVE AGREEMENT WITH EVERLINK SERVICES
- EASYPARK SIGNS WITH MINT INC. TO OFFER CUSTOMERS WIRELESS PAYMENT OPTIONS
- ICAO LOOKS TO THE EMV EXPERIENCE
- KEYCORP TERMINALS IN CANADIAN MERCHANT DEPLOYMENT
- KEYCORP TO SUPPLY TERMINALS FOR CANADIAN BUSINESS REWARDS PROGRAM
- LASERCARD GETS $1.8 MILLION ORDER FOR CANADIAN PERMANENT RESIDENT CARD PROGRAM
- MASTERCARD & VISA TO RELEASE JOINT EMV SMART CARD PERSONALIZATION SPECS
- MILLIONS OF CANADIANS TO GET A COMPUTER ON THEIR VISA CARD – THE EMV ANNOUNCEMENT
- NEW BENEFIT FOR ACT CANADA MEMBERS
- QUNARA WINS SECURITY SERVICES CONTRACT TO SUPPLY ONTARIO

- GOVERNMENT'S 'SMART SYSTEMS FOR HEALTH' PROGRAM
- RBC ROYAL BANK LAUNCHES CANADA'S FIRST NATIONAL VISA CHIP CARD
- SUN & EDS ADDRESS DEMAND FOR HEIGHTENED INFORMATION SECURITY WITH SMART CARD SOLUTIONS FOR CANADIAN GOV'T
- TELE-CHEQUES TO BE PROHIBITED IN CANADIAN CLEARING SYSTEM
- VISA TO ISSUE PASSWORDS THROUGH CANADIAN BANKS

Canadian news

2002 Key highlights...

- ACT Canada helped issuers and other members reach the same point, subject to their timetables and budgets, by facilitating convergence
  This includes:
  - promoting awareness and acceptance of standards
  - fostering partnerships and other working relationships
  - building an educated and enthusiastic marketplace
  - being a key influencer of stakeholders
- Through the launch of the member driven National Issuers & Infrastructure Committee and other services, ACT Canada helped members focus on:
  - how a national smart card infrastructure could be leveraged
  - the role of smart cards in identity management and cyber-terrorism

Metrics

- 12 member events / workgroups
- 37+ publications / reports /papers
- 18 speeches / briefings
- 12 government consultations / appointments, key interactions

The market...

- In 2002, Canadian financial institutions start to seriously investigate and issue smart cards, after years of conjecture that mobile phones would negate the need for chip cards
- Canadian online banking doubles over 2 years
- Various provincial and federal government groups also look at ways to use the security of smart cards in a post 9-11 environment
- Identity theft is a rapidly growing issue
- Smart card shipments to U.S. & Canada doubles in 1st half of 2002

Board of Directors

Douglas Beardshaw	Devmark
Bob Cheriton	Insight Navigation
Martyn Cooper	MasterCard
Chris Gray	SchlumbergerSema
Ed Gresham	Giesecke & Devrient
Catherine Johnston	ACT Canada
Jayson Rainone	TD CT
Allen Wright	Visa Canada

ACT Canada notes of interest

- 13 radio interviews in 24 hours when the Auditor General of Canada reports on social insurance number fraud
- ACT Canada becomes charter member of the International Smart Card Associations Network (ISCAN)
- Code of Ethics introduced for all ACT Canada members to build market confidence
- Membership grew even though many members stopped doing business in Canada

2002

Bringing members together and building an informed market

ACT Canada Member Events, Teams and Workgroups	Publications, Reports, Papers & Media	Speeches, Briefings
• Advanced Card Technology 101 seminar • Annual General Meeting • Awards • Cyber-Terrorism Symposium • E-terrorism and Protecting Your Customer's Privacy Symposium • Infrastructure Forum • Market Intelligence Roundtable • National Issuers & Infrastructure Committee launched • Network and Education meeting • Retail Forum • Secure ID Symposium • Trusted Registrations for Secure IDs symposium	• *A New Partnership Approach to Business Applications, Infrastructure and Application Development Whitepaper* National Issuers & Infrastructure Committee • *ACTion news* (11 editions) • *Business Rationale for PKI / Smart Card rollout Whitepaper* National Issuers & Infrastructure Committee • *Consumer and Corporate Users Whitepaper* National Issuers & Infrastructure Committee • Coverage of the ACT Canada Security symposium by CTV, CBC, Global & 680 News • *Design Considerations - A Business Perspective* National Issuers & Infrastructure Committee: • *Identity Theft – are you at risk?* for ICMA • *Identity Theft – are you at risk?* Luggage, Leathergoods and Accessories magazine • *Identity theft* CH Morning Live • *Infrastructure Whitepaper* National Issuers & Infrastructure Committee • *Issues Position Paper* • *Market Survey to identify issues* for the purposes of building solutions • *Members Directory* • New York Times – responded to incorrect article on smart card security • *Ontario smart card project review* • *Privacy and Security - the Balancing Point* SCTI journal • *Privacy Whitepaper* National Issuers & Infrastructure Committee	• 11th Annual Card Manufacturing Expo 2002 - Advanced Card workshop • ACT Canada's first Market Intelligence Roundtable – speaker • Advanced Card Technology Seminars – instructor • Cyber-Terrorism Symposium • *E-Terrorism and Protecting Your Customer's Privacy – How to protect your customer's privacy – a tutorial* • *E-Terrorism and Protecting Your Customer's Privacy - National Infrastructure briefing* • *Identity theft and Cyber-terrorism* Mississauga Technology Association • *Identity theft: you are at risk (keynote)* The Mississauga Board of Trade • *Identity Theft: you are at risk* ICMA • *Identity theft: you are at risk* Kitchener Westmount Rotary Club • Ontario Smart Card Review • Privacy and Identity Theft Symposium • *Smart Card 101 – Security, Access Control, Authentication, Payment, Stored Value and Loyalty….*Citysoup.ca Innovation Centre BC • *Smart Choices* Industry Canada • Technology in Government - panel • *Terrorism, Privacy And Trade, What Do They Have In Common?* International Trade Club of Toronto • *The Ontario Smart Card Project: a PIA* ACT Canada review

Publications, Reports, Papers & Media	Speeches, Briefings (continued)
- *Register of existing projects (Canadian & International)*	- Trusted Registrations for Secure IDs symposium
- *Securing the Nation's Borders: A Practical and Economical Approach* LaserCard Systems Corporation	
- Security and Privacy interviews – CBC TV, CBC Radio, QR77 radio	
- Security Products and Technology News	
- *Security Whitepaper* National Issuers & Infrastructure Committee	
- *Technology in Government interview on the role of smart cards to protect citizens and consumers*	
- The Computer Paper	
- The Edge	
- *What is identity theft?*	
- *White Paper on Border Security*	

Key Additional Member Services	External Events (other)
- CPA e-funds discussions	- CardTech/SecurTech
- Business Opportunity Bulletins	- Cartes
- Professional Development Program	- Smart Card Alliance
- Discount for advertising in InfoSystems and Technology in Government	- Technology in Government Week, Ottawa (GTech)

Government Appointments	Government Key Consultations
▪ Canadian Payments Association - Stakeholders Advisory Council, Vice Chair (3 year appointment by the Minister of Finance)	▪ Belgium trade commission meeting ▪ Citizenship and Immigration Canada national ID card consultation ▪ Government of Canada marketplace status briefing ▪ Indian and Northern Affairs Canada (INAC) requests help with the Status Card ▪ Industry Canada – Smart Choices ▪ Ministry of Business and Consumer Services (Ont) requests meeting to discuss security, biometrics and chips + ACT met with ministry reps and a California delegation responsible for Citizen's registrations ▪ Network of Excellence for Sustainable Transportation- Moving the Economy discussion on skilled resources requirements ▪ Office of Consumer Awareness discussion on smart cards for EFT ▪ Province of Ontario (various ministries) – debriefing on previous government attempts to move to chip based health cards. ▪ Survey for Moving the Economy ▪ Treasury Board Secretariat of Canada - Smart Card Standards Analysis

and in the...

- 1ST CAMPUS SMART CARD AUTOMATION SYSTEM IN BC
- ACT CANADA LAUNCHES 2002 MEMBERSHIP DRIVE & EVERYONE WINS!
- ACT CANADA MEMBERSHIP ELECTS 2003 BOARD OF DIRECTORS
- ACT CANADA: MAKING SOLUTIONS POSSIBLE
- ACT EVENT CONFIRMS ISSUERS INTEREST IN MOVING FORWARD SMART CARDS PLANS
- AIROS GROUP AWARDED PRODUCT DEVELOPMENT CONTRACT
- ALL-PURPOSE CHIPS ARE FINALLY IN THE CARDS
- BMO LAUNCHES MOSAIK MASTERCARD
- CANADA CUSTOMS TO USE IRIS SCANS AT AIRPORTS
- CANADIAN BANK NOTE COMPANY LTD CO-DESIGNS PERMANENT RESIDENT CARD
- CATHERINE JOHNSTON & KENNETH WONG TO KEYNOTE ICMA'S 11TH ANNUAL CARD MANUFACTURING EXPO
- CDN ONLINE BANKING DOUBLES OVER TWO YEARS
- CIBC & AMEX LAUNCH CANADA'S 1ST NATIONAL SMART CREDIT CARD
- CITY OF TORONTO AWARDED FUNDING TO STUDY SMART CARDS
- COBRANDING KEY TO AMEX'S CANADIAN PLANS
- CUBIC WINS EDMONTON TRANSIT SYSTEM CONTRACT
- DATAKEY EXPANDS ITS BUSINESS WITH THE CANADIAN GOV'T
- IDENTITY THEFT GROWING AT ALARMING RATE
- INDUSTRY PRESSURES TO USE SMART CARDS IN AVIATION SECURITY
- INTERAC DIRECT PAYMENT IS #1 AGAIN
- KASYS INT'L OPENS KASYS CANADA

- KINGSTON BIA & SCOTIABANK INTRODUCE SMART LOYALTY PROGRAM
- MARKET UPDATE FROM ACT CANADA
- MASTERCARD & VISA REACH ACCORD ON INTERNET SECURITY
- MIST EXPANDS WITH THE OPENING OF ASIA-PACIFIC OFFICE
- ONTARIO CUTS `SMART CARD' SYSTEM AFTER SPENDING MILLIONS
- ONTARIO SMART CARD PROJECT INSIGHTS ADDED TO MARCH 18TH SYMPOSIUM
- PLANNING THE CANADIAN INFRASTRUCTURE
- SMART CARD GROUPS FORM GLOBAL NETWORK
- SMART CARD SHIPMENTS TO U.S. & CANADA DOUBLES IN 1ST HALF OF 2002
- SMART CARD VULNERABILITY?

Canadian news

2001 Key highlights...

- Through 4 member driven workgroups and other services, ACT Canada helped members focus on:
  - EMV, merchant and government issues and opportunities
  - other market issues and opportunities
- Assisted members in developing new offerings, competitive strategies and reduced time to market

Metrics

- 15 member events and workgroups
- 27 publications/reports/papers
- 14 speeches
- 6 Professional Development events
- 12 government consultations / appointments, key interactions
- 18 graduates of the Professional Development Program and 27 additional working towards graduation

The market...

- In 2001, the Canadian smart card market heats up
- Visa Canada announces that they are going chip!
- Canadian financial institutions launch new smart card initiatives, some partnering with city and provincial government groups
- US & Canada Smart Card Survey Shows Usage Surged 37% in 2000
- The Northern Friends Rewards Program. It is the largest North American program to utilize smart card technology in a loyalty/customer relationship application
- Security applications are high profile after 9/11

Board of Directors

Douglas Beardshaw	Devmark
Eric Beaudin	Gemplus Canada
Joanne Boyar	
Brian Brett	Oasis Technology Ltd.
Linda Copland	VanCity Saving Credit Union
Alain J. Cusson	Bell Canada
John Ellis	Credit Union Central of Canada
Johanne T Ghali	American Express Canada Inc
Ed Gresham	Giesecke & Devrient
Richard T. Hauge	Smart Chip Technologies
Joanne Heward	American Express
Catherine Johnston	ACT Canada
Ken Kivenko	Kenmar
Anne Lawrence	Compaq Canada
Greg McKenzie	Metaca Corporation
David Phillips	Mondex Canada Association
Sharon Radford	Xansa
Jim Warnock	I V I Checkmate Ltd
Allen Wright	Visa Canada Association

ACT Canada notes of interest

- ACT moves to new offices due to staff growth
- The annual conference is branded Cardware
- A member code of ethics is introduced to build market confidence in our members

2001

Bringing members together and building an informed market

ACT Canada Member Events, Teams and Workgroups	Publications, Reports, Papers & Media	Speeches
- Annual General Meeting - Awards - Cardware seminars - EMV seminar - EMV Workgroup - FIs meet with Ontario Smart Card project representatives - Government Workgroup formed by federal and provincial governments and payment stakeholders - National Infrastructure Forum launched - National Merchants Forum (workgroup) launched - Network and Education meetings (6) - Retail workgroup launched - Retailer Forum - Ride the Wave conference (ACT Canada/CTST) - Secure Commerce in a "Multi-Channel, Multi-Service" Delivery Environment lunch - Secure ID Symposium	- *2nd Financial Post supplement published: Smart Card Technologies* - ACTion news (11 editions) - Advanced Cards 101 – a primer - *An Introduction to EMV: The Smart Card Industry Standard -* Ingenico - *Cashless Society* - *Current Canadian Projects review* - *Electronic Fraud: Privacy and Security* - *In your wallet today: personal information at risk* - *Members Directory* - *Ontario Position Paper: Smart Benefits Card* - *Privacy and Security: where do we go now?* - *Privacy and Smart Cards* - *Privacy and Smart Cards* Globe and Mail - *Smart Card Technology: Ecstasy and Elephant Traps* - *Smart Cards for Smart Consumers whitepaper* Frontier Strategies - *The Canadian Smart Card Market review* SCTI journal - Canada was the focus country - *What are advanced card technologies: 2 Cdn projects*	- Cardware seminars - *Electronic Cash in Canada: Lessons Learned* Federal Reserve Bank of Chicago - EMV Course - instructor - EMV seminar - *Is there a role for smart cards? panelist* Canadian Payments Association conference - *Privacy and Smart Cards* Cardware 2001 - Ride the Wave conference (ACT Canada/CTST) - *Secure Commerce in a "Multi-Channel, Multi-Service" Delivery Environment* - Secure ID Symposium - Smart Card Industry Association speech - *Smart Cards – Ecstasy and Elephant Traps* ICMA conference - *Smart cards - The inevitable e-commerce enabler* Ottawa Centre for Research and Innovation - *Smart Cards – today and tomorrow* Canadian Payments Association conference Emerging Technology Policy workgroup - *Smart cards and security* Security.net 2001

Key Additional Member Services	External Events (other)
<ul><li>ACT negotiates substantial discounts for member ads in Card Technology magazine and SCTI Journal</li><li>Advised on new legislations and ensured that there was no bias against advanced cards</li><li>Linked members with media post 9-11 to talk about secure ID</li><li>Member Code of Ethics introduced</li><li>Members' directory enhanced on web site</li><li>Professional Development Program – Cdn first in this field</li><li>Successfully fought against the introduction of regulations and legislation that would have restricted the introduction and use of the technology</li></ul>	<ul><li>CardTech/SecurTech</li></ul>

Government Appointments	Government Key Consultations	Government Key Interactions
<ul><li>Canadian Payments Association – Stakeholders Advisory Council</li><li>Management Board Secretariat (Ont) - Ontario Smart Card Project External Advisory Council</li></ul>	<ul><li>Citizenship and Immigration Canada national ID card consultation</li><li>Government of Canada marketplace status briefing</li><li>HRDC re requirements for training programs to support market employment needs</li><li>Ministry of Business and Consumer Services (Ont) requests meeting to discuss security, biometrics and chips + ACT met with ministry reps and a California delegation responsible for Citizen's registrations</li><li>Network of Excellence for Sustainable Transportation-Moving the Economy discussion on skilled resources requirements</li><li>Office of Consumer Awareness discussion on smart cards for EFT</li><li>Province of Ontario (various ministries) – debriefing on previous government attempts to move to chip based health cards.</li><li>Survey for Moving the Economy</li><li>Treasury Board Secretariat of Canada - Smart Card Standards Analysis</li></ul>	<ul><li>Industry Canada asks ACT to facilitate a meeting with payment stakeholders</li></ul>

and in the...

- ACT CANADA ANNOUNCES NEW INFRASTRUCTURE & RETAILER FORUMS
- ACT CANADA APPLAUDS THE ONTARIO GOVERNMENT'S PLANS TO USE SMART CARDS
- ACT CANADA PRESENTS THE SECURE ID SYMPOSIUM
- ACT CANADA TO HOST EMV WORKGROUP IN JUNE
- B.C. TRYING TO BEAT HEALTH-CARE FRAUD SMART CARD, INTERNET MAY BE USED IN FIGHT
- BRITISH GOV'T DEPARTMENT TRIALS DIGITAL SIGNATURE TECHNOLOGY
- CANADA TRIES " SMART CARDS " TO BEAT IMMIGRATION FRAUD
- CANADA'S FIRST REGIONAL LOYALTY PROGRAM LAUNCHED
- CANADIAN MARKETPLACE HEATS UP
- CANADIAN VISA CARDS TO GET CHIPS
- COINAMATIC PARTNERS WITH EDGEWARE
- DOWNTOWN KINGSTON! BUSINESS IMPROVEMENT ASSOCIATION AND SCOTIABANK PARTNER TO INTRODUCE A NEW LOYALTY SMART CARD PROGRAM
- EXOCOM & DATAKEY TO DELIVER PKI SMART CARD SYSTEMS TO CDN. DEPARTMENT OF NATIONAL DEFENCE
- INDUSTRY EXPERTS TO CONVERGE UPON TORONTO
- IVI CHECKMATE WIRELESS TRANSACTION TERMINALS TO BE USED IN COINAMATIC LAUNDRY ROOMS THROUGHOUT CANADA
- METACA ACQUIRES NBS CANADA
- OASIS TECHNOLOGY, SILVERLINE, GIESECKE & DEVRIENT, INGENICO, SMART CHIP TECHNOLOGIES & CARDIS TO DEVELOP MULTI-APPLICATION SMART CARD SUITE
- PRESIDENT'S CHOICE FINANCIAL MASTERCARD CHOOSES PARTNERS TO LAUNCH CREDIT CARD

- PRIVACY MANAGEMENT & COMPLIANCE: THE TIP OF THE ICEBERG
- PROLIFIC TECHNOLOGY - PURCHASE ORDER FOR UNIVERSITY OF ALBERTA - STUDENTS' UNION GAMES ROOM
- QI & TELUS DEVELOP SMART CARD PAYMENT TERMINALS
- QUICK FACTS & STATS
- RONALD MCDONALD NOW WIRELESS?
- SCOTIABANK ADDS DEBIT FEATURE TO CHIP PILOT
- SCOTIABANK DELIVERS FIRST ALL-IN-ONE MICROCHIP CARD SOLUTION WITH SOLSTICE
- SMART CARDS -- INTEROPERABILITY IS THE KEY
- SMART CARDS WILL HELP TOURISTS GET MEDICAL CARE
- UNIVERSITY OF OTTAWA IMPLEMENTS SMART CARD PROGRAM
- UPCOMING ACT CANADA LUNCHEON: SECURE COMMERCE IN A "MULTI-CHANNEL, MULTI-SERVICE" DELIVERY ENVIRONMENT
- US & CANADA SMART CARD SURVEY SHOWS USAGE SURGED 37% IN 2000

Canadian news

2000 Key highlights...

- Through member education and other services, ACT Canada helped members focus on:
  - EMV in the Canadian context
  - E-delivery of financial services
  - market issues and opportunities

Metrics

- 8 member events plus
- 6 Professional Development events
- 19 publications/reports/papers
- 16 speeches, briefings
- 7 government consultations / appointments, key interactions

The market...

- Interac, MasterCard and Visa standards identify unique Canadian requirements while staying compliant with EMV
- Mondex Canada Surpasses $2 Million Mark In E-Cash Issuance and introduces a debit and e-cash card in Sherbrooke
- Scotiabank has 40k VISACash cards and 600 merchants in Barrie
- Transit, loyalty and prepaid continue to be the dominant areas for smart cards, but the financial sector is paying attention to EMV
- Ontario is the first province to publicly commit to smart cards
- Quebec reaffirms their intention to introduce a chip based health card

Board of Directors

Douglas Beardshaw	Devmark Technology Management
Joyce Bodner	Diesel Farms
Joanne Boyar	RBA Inc
Martyn Cooper	Royal Bank
Joanne De Laurentiis	Mondex Canada
John Ellis	Credit Union Central Canada
Johanne T Ghali	American Express Canada Inc
Ed Gresham	G & D Security Card Systems Inc
Martin Hemy	I V I Checkmate Ltd
Catherine Johnston	ACT Canada
Anne Lawrence	ACI Worldwide (Canada) Inc
Greg McKenzie	Metaca Corporation
Doug Melville	CIBC
Tracy Norman	Tracy Norman & Associates
Sharon Radford	Duhig Berry Inc.
Donna Rougeau	JAWS Technologies Inc
Allen Wright	BIT Intergations Inc.

... and on the executive committee...

Linda Copland	VanCity Credit Union
Rich Hauge	OSI
Walt Lemon	Visa Canada

ACT Canada notes of interest

- Information and Privacy Commissioner Ontario (IPCO) works with ACT Canada to develop the world's first the Privacy Impact Assessment Procedure for multi-application card systems
- ACT Canada prepares to provide member support for EMV
- New association products and services are announced

2000

Bringing members together and building an informed market

ACT Canada Member Events, Teams and Workgroups	Publications, Reports, Papers & Media	Speeches, Briefings
▪ ACT (CTST) Catch the Wave Conference ▪ Annual General Meeting ▪ Awards ▪ Market Intelligence program launched ▪ Membership Appreciation reception ▪ Multi-App 101 seminar ▪ Network and Education meetings (6) ▪ Smart Cards 101 seminar ▪ Professional Development Program launched	▪ *2000 Canadian Smart Card Project list* ▪ *A Move Towards A Cashless Canada* The Treasurer ▪ *ACTion bulletins (11 editions)* (Note: the news goes electronic!) ▪ *Canadian Business Week* supplement on the trends, issues and opportunities of the Canadian advanced card technology market ▪ *Focus on Canada* Card Technology Magazine ▪ Members Directory ▪ *Multi-Application Smart Cards: How to do a Privacy Assessment* co-authored with Information and Privacy Commission, Ontario ▪ *Security and Smart Cards* ▪ *Smart Card, Optical and Other Advanced Cards: How to do a Privacy Assessment* world's first PIA for this technology, co-authored with IPC/O	▪ *Business line opportunities related to smart cards* Ottawa Centre for Research and Innovation (Ottawa) ▪ *Canadian Payment Strategies in a New Environment* The Strategy Institute - Creating a New Business Synergy ▪ *Check Fraud and Smart Cards* NACHA Electronic Check Council ▪ CTST Canada ▪ *e-Delivery of financial services* CCECE 2000 ▪ *e-delivery of financial services* Infonex ▪ *Multi-App 101* ▪ *Online Payments: Challenges and Opportunities (panel moderator)* Federal Reserve Bank of Chicago Promoting the Use of Electronic Payments: Considering Future Requirements (Chicago) ▪ *Smart Cards - Surviving the e-business transformation* Electronic Commerce Canada ▪ *Smart cards and the Canadian market* with Joanne De Laurentiis, Royal Canadian Mint Board ▪ *Smart Cards* Payments Association ▪ *Smart Cards, Privacy and the Government* Strategy Institute Personal Health Information Update (Toronto) ▪ *Smart cards: ecstasy and elephant traps* ICMA ▪ *Smart Cards: the sizzling security solution for e-commerce* IEEE ▪ *Smart credit, debit and cash: Understanding why Canada is so far ahead of the United States* E-Delivery of Financial

- Services (Toronto)
- *The challenges of rolling out smart bank cards* Canadian Payments Association, Emerging Payments Technology Group

Key Additional Member Services

- ACTing on your behalf program launched
- C Johnston is invited to represent ACT Canada members on the International Biometrics Industry Association advisory board
- Consulting services
- Market research subscriptions launched
- Professional Development Program launched
- The association pushes back on a National Post story

External Events (other)

- CardTech/SecurTech

Government Appointments

- Canadian Payments Association - Stakeholders Advisory Council
- Minister of Management Board Secretariat (Ont) – appoints ACT Canada to the Ontario Smart Card Project External Advisory Council

Government Key Consultations

- Consultation: Proposed Ontario Privacy ACT
- Information and Privacy Commissioner Ontario (IPCO) works with ACT Canada to develop the world's first the Privacy Impact Assessment Procedure for multi-application card systems
- Management Board Secretariat (Ont) research requests
- Management Board Secretariat and Ministry of Health (Ont) briefings for ADM and government officials re smart health cards

Government Key Interactions

- Management Board Secretariat (Ont) requests that we substitute for them as a speaker at a Health Privacy Legislation conference

- ACT CANADA NETWORK & EDUCATION GROUP MEETING SCHEDULE RELEASED
- ACT CANADA TO ANNOUNCE NEW PRODUCTS AND SERVICES AT CARDTECH/SECURTECH, MIAMI
- ACT CANADA'S MARCH NETWORK AND EDUCATION GROUP LUNCHEON SELLS OUT!
- CANADA COMMITS TO EMV (JUNE)
- CANADIAN CITY TO GET LOYALTY SMART CARD
- CANADIAN GOV'T TO ISSUE 2.3 MILLION OPTICAL CARDS
- DUPONT CANADA, MDC CORPORATION, BATTELLE AND CROWN INVESTMENTS CORPORATION INVEST IN PRIMAXIS TECHNOLOGY VENTURES INC. TO BUILD ADVANCED TECHNOLOGY COMPANIES
- EARLYRAIN INC INSTALLS MAJOR SMART CARD SYSTEM AT CALGARY'S GLENCOE CLUB
- EMV WORKSHOPS TO BE RUN MID-JUNE IN TORONTO
- G&D AND CIT TEAM UP TO BRING LEADING SMART CARD E-COMMERCE SOLUTIONS TO NORTH AMERICA
- GROWING FRAUD PUSHING CANADIANS TOWARD SMART CARDS
- IDSHIELD ONLINE BANKING & E-PAYMENT AUTHENTICATION SYSTEM HELPS ELIMINATE USER IDENTITY THEFT
- MDC'S METACA PARTNERS WITH SYMCOR
- MONDEX CANADA SURPASSES $2 MILLION MARK IN E-CASH ISSUANCE
- MONDEX™ E-CASH PROGRAM GENERATES TECHNOLOGICAL INNOVATIONS
- NBS AND VISA OFFER SMART CARD DEAL TO BANKS
- RECORD NUMBERS ATTEND CARDTECH/SECURTECH CANADA 2000, CATCH THE WAVE
- SCOTIABANK BUILDS A COMBINATION TRANSIT AND LOYALTY CARD

Canadian news

1999 Key highlights...

■ Through member education, market briefings and other services, ACT Canada helped members focus on emerging market opportunities, barriers and issues

Metrics

- ❑ 23 member events and workgroups
- ❑ 15 publications/reports/papers
- ❑ 16 speeches, briefings
- ❑ 16 government consultations / appointments, key interactions

The market...

- ❑ There is significant government activity at all levels
- ❑ The financial sector starts to talk about a cashless society and looks at various card applications, but many suggest that payment will "leapfrog over smart cards and go to mobile phones"
- ❑ The market moves from curiosity to planning
- ❑ Visa, MasterCard, American Express and others issue common security standards for smart cards
- ❑ The world's first multi-currency cross-border e-purse transaction happens
- ❑ Ontario is the first province to commit to smart cards
- ❑ Loyalty and prepayment applications continue to lead the market
- ❑ Mondex Canada launches a combination "debit and Mondex e-cash card"
- ❑ Resources that were temporarily assigned to Y2K projects had a window of opportunity in the latter half of the year to return to card related planning
- ❑ The federal government looks at new SIN cards and asks ACT Canada to participate
- ❑ The Federal Government evaluates smart cards for:
    - ❑ Portable digital certificates
    - ❑ E-commerce
    - ❑ Potential national I.D. card to replace current S.I.N. cards
    - ❑ Access to the Internet
    - ❑ And many other applications

Board of Directors

Doug Beardshaw	HP/Verifone
Joyce Bodner	Diesel Farms
Joanne Boyar	RBA Inc
Martyn Cooper	Royal Bank
Linda Copland	VanCity Credit Union
Joanne DeLaurentiis	Mondex
Paul DeRosse	Verifone Ltd
John Ellis	CUCC
Peter Everill	CIBC
Dawn Gallagher	BA Custom Cards
Ed Gresham	G & D Security Card Systems
Rich Hauge	OSI
Martin Hemy	I V I Checkmate Ltd
Wendy Hope	Canadian Payments Association
Catherine Johnston	ACT Canada
Murray Johnston	Amdahl – Smart Card Group
Greg McKenzie	Metaca Corporation
Doug Melville	CIBC
Garry Morehouse	Visa Canada
Sharon Radford	Duhig Berry
Allen Wright	BIT Integrations

ACT Canada notes of interest

- Faulkner & Gray and ACT Canada announce the first CardTech/SecurTech Canada to be held in Toronto, August 24th – 26th
- produces the world's first Halloween themed smart (prepaid) card
- formally protests to CBC over misleading Mondex and privacy coverage
- launches Smart Card Education Group - monthly meetings
- upgrades ACTion news from print to electronic delivery

1999

Bringing members together and building an informed market

ACT Canada Member Events, Teams and Workgroups	Publications, Reports, Papers & Media	Speeches, Briefings
<ul><li>ACT (CTST) Celebrating the Successes Conference (Toronto)</li><li>Annual General Meeting</li><li>Cardware 99: Smart Cards, State of the Art, Ottawa</li><li>Cardware thank you reception</li><li>Celebrating the Successes Awards</li><li>Corporate briefings day (Ottawa)</li><li>Education workgroup lunch and learn series: card fraud in Canada and around the world (+ 10 additional meetings)</li><li>Executive Breakfast Briefing: APACS (Toronto)</li><li>Executive Briefing Seminar (Ottawa)</li><li>Innovators Briefing Seminar (Ottawa)</li><li>Meeting of international organizations in Toronto to discuss successful stakeholder management practices</li><li>Retailers work group meetings</li><li>Smart Cards 101 training</li></ul>	<ul><li>ACT Canada ACTing on Your Behalf news (4 editions + 1st electronic)</li><li>*ACT CANADA Advanced Card Technology Glossary of Terms Version 2.0*</li><li>*Canada: Catch the Wave*</li><li>*Canadian Market Trends* SCTI journal</li><li>Canadian Parliamentary Standing Committee of Human Rights and Persons with Disabilities - submission on *the management of a new Social Insurance Number card*</li><li>*Market Intelligence reports*</li><li>*Members Directory*</li><li>*Ontario government smart card: What will it mean for you?*</li><li>*Privacy and Advanced Card Technology: privacy and e-commerce*</li><li>*The Canadian advanced card project list*</li><li>Work starts on the world's first *Privacy Impact Assessment Procedure for Multi-Application Cards* sponsored by ACT Canada and the Information and Privacy Commissioner, Ontario.</li></ul>	<ul><li>ACT (CTST) Celebrating the Successes Conference</li><li>*Balancing Data Distribution with Data Protection* Comdex (Montreal)</li><li>Cards 101 workshop Comdex</li><li>Cardware 99</li><li>Corporate Briefings - Ottawa</li><li>*E-Business and Smart Cards - A Marriage of Convenience panel moderator* Electronic Commerce Canada</li><li>Executive Seminar - Ottawa</li><li>*Hardware, Software and now…* Smart Card Technology Institute launch</li><li>Innovators Briefing Seminar</li><li>*Moving Toward a Cashless Society keynote* TMAC</li><li>*Multi-Application Cards* a presentation to the External Advisory Council (Gov of Ont)</li><li>*Privacy and Advanced Card Technology: Privacy and eCommerce* IEEE Conference -</li><li>*Smart Cards – On the Road to a Cashless Society moderator* Canadian Payments Association Conference</li><li>Smart Cards 101</li><li>*Smart Cards in Canada* Cartes (Paris)</li><li>*The changing landscape of payments in Canada* Federal Reserve Bank of Chicago</li></ul>

Key Additional Member Services	External Events (other)
▪ A market briefing is provided for a new biometric company ▪ ACT Canada assists members with personnel recruitment ▪ ACT Canada has been requested to provide executive briefing sessions for several members. ▪ ACT is represented on ISO Canadian Advisory Committee ▪ Consulting for members on a multi-application card system ▪ Co-sponsored ACI's Retailer's Day ▪ Developed Executive Insight program for Smart Card Technology Institute ▪ Global Stored Value Supplier Program ▪ Professional Development Program ▪ University of Toronto approaches ACT Canada as a research partner ▪ Worked with Amdahl to plan the launch of the SmartCard Institute	▪ ACT Canada co-ordinates a meeting of international organizations in Toronto to discuss successful stakeholder management practices. ▪ CardTech/SecurTech Chicago ▪ CardTech/SecurTech East ▪ CardTech/SecurTech West ▪ Global Chip Card Alliance meeting (Long Beach) ▪ MAOSCO meeting (Miami) ▪ President reviewed the VIP Toronto smart card program and provided comments on the program and roll out ▪ Smart Card Technology Institute launch

Government Appointments	Government Key Consultations	Government Key Interactions
▪ Canadian Payments Association – Stakeholders Advisory Council , Vice Chair ▪ Management Board Secretariat Smart Card External Advisory Council (Ont) member	▪ A Presentation to the External Advisory Council (Gov of Ont) - Multi-Application Cards ▪ Canadian Parliamentary Standing Committee of Human Rights and Persons with Disabilities - testimony on the management of a new Social Insurance Number card – included a suggested solution to the problem as mentioned by the Auditor General and a funding mechanism ▪ Competition Bureau asks for information about Mondex ▪ Industry Canada briefing on new market advances as they move to pilot their Community Access (Internet) Program ▪ Ministry of Consumer and Commercial Relations (Ont) to advise on methodologies and stakeholder management for the Open Business Connect program ▪ Ministry of Consumer and Commercial Relations Ontario – consulting on Open Business Connect program ▪ Ministry of Health (Ontario) consulting ▪ RCMP Proceeds of Crime Branch requests information on smart cards and other financial payment issues. ▪ Royal Canadian Mint briefing for the board of directors, executive committee and senior management on the emergence of advanced cards as payment mechanisms. ▪ VIP Toronto smart card program review	▪ ACT receives a partnership request forwarded by the British Trade Commission ▪ Industry Canada meetings to advise on the use of smart cards for the new federal community (internet) access program ▪ Industry Canada's Community Access Program team meeting ▪ University of Toronto approaches ACT Canada as a research partner.

and in the first electronic version of the ACTion news, November 1999

- ACT CANADA AND FAULKNER & GRAY ANNOUNCE PLANS FOR CARDTECH/SECURTECH CANADA 2000 "CATCH THE WAVE"
- ACT CANADA LAUNCHES INDUSTRY RESEARCH INITIATIVE
- BULL ANNOUNCES "CRYPTO SAFE" SMART CARDS
- ERG TRANSIT SYSTEM TO BE IMPLEMENTED IN UK
- MULTOS CHOSEN AS PLATFORM FOR MULTI-APPLICATION SMART CARDS IN AUSTRALIA
- ONTARIO AND QUEBEC ANNOUNCE SMART CARD INITIATIVES
- SMART CARD COMMERCE TO BE LAUNCHED
- SMART CARD LOYALTY APPLICATIONS USED TO KEEP KIDS IN SCHOOL
- SMART CARD SECURITY STANDARDS ADDRESSED
- THE WORLD'S FIRST MULTI-CURRENCY, CROSS BORDER E-PURSE TRANSACTION

Canadian news

1998 Key highlights...

ACT Canada helped members understand the emerging payments and travel applications by bringing together stakeholder groups in meetings, workgroups and other educational events. The association's mission is to inform, advocate and educate.

Metrics

- 24 member events and workgroups
- 14 publications/reports/papers
- 19 speeches / briefings
- 12 government consultations / appointments, key interactions

The market...

- Mondex led the activity in the financial sector wrapping up the Guelph trial and moving to Sherbrooke Quebec in '99
- There is international interest from European FIs in how Canada is progressing with smart cards
- Interest broadens as airlines and entertainment groups look at the potential of smart cards
- Credit card fraud grows significantly
- Y2K drains resources from potential payment applications
- Montreal pilots a parking payment contactless solution
- Bell Canada's QuickChange card continues to be a popular stored value application
- Consumer field trial of Visa Cash in Barrie
- The first multi-purpose chip card in Canada at an educational institution

Board of Directors

Joyce Bodner	Deisel Farms
Joanne Boyar	RBA Inc
Wendy Cartwright	Royal Bank
Garry Caughlin	Caughlin and Associates
Martyn Cooper	Royal Bank
Joanne De Laurentiis	Mondex Canada
Paul De Rosse	Verifone
John Ellis	Credit Union Central of Canada
Dawn Gallagher	BA Custom Cards
Wendy Hope	Canadian Payments Association
Catherine Johnston	ACT Canada
Greg McKenzie	MDC Card Services
Pam Peck	Visa Canada Association
Ralph Sutton	Blackhall Smartech Inc
Peter Uehlecke	SGS Thomson

ACT Canada notes of interest

- The Discovery Channel shoots a segment for @Discovery on the future of smart cards at the ACT office
- Members' web forum launched
- Annual awards program launched
- The office moves out of Catherine Johnston's home to accommodate a growing staff
- Andrea McMullen joins ACT Canada's staff
- The annual conference is branded Cardware
- Agreement reached with CardTech/SecurTech for a joint venture in Canada

1998

Bringing members together and building an informed market

ACT Canada Member Events, Teams and Workgroups	Publications, Reports, Papers & Media	Speeches, Briefings
<ul><li>An introduction to Advanced Card Technologies Seminar for the Canadian Information Processing Society (CIPS) (Vancouver and Victoria)</li><li>2 meetings of the Global Stored Value Suppliers Forum (formerly the Mondex Suppliers forum)</li><li>Annual General Meeting</li><li>Awards ceremony</li><li>Introduction to Advanced Card Technologies seminar (Toronto)</li><li>Mondex Suppliers meeting (Washington)</li><li>Privacy Seminar (Toronto)</li><li>Racing to the Future with Smart Cards Conference (Toronto)</li><li>Retailers Symposium on New Payment Systems</li><li>Retailers, bankers and technologists brought together to discuss the evolving payment system in Canada</li><li>Smart Card Education Work Group (monthly lunch and learns)</li><li>Smart Cards - Where do you start? Workshop</li><li>Smart Cards '98 Seminar (Toronto)</li></ul>	<ul><li>*1 year review of Mondex trial* CBC @discovery</li><li>ACTion newsletter</li><li>Advanced Card Privacy Assessment Checklist with IPC/O</li><li>Canada: Another Big Year in Smart Cards SCTI journal</li><li>CKNW Vancouver – Money Talks show</li><li>CTV news – card fraud</li><li>CTV news – Mondex and Visa Cash</li><li>*Financial Post Supplement: It's all in the smart cards! (2nd annual publication)*</li><li>*Industry Directory*</li><li>Kitchener Record</li><li>*Members Directory*</li><li>*The Canadian Market* European Card Review</li><li>*Web forums* launched for Telephony Special Interest Group, Mondex Unattended Point of Sale SIG and Global Stored Value Supplier Group</li><li>*What is the right to privacy with respect to non-internet applications (technology of privacy or technology of surveillance?)*</li></ul>	<ul><li>An introduction to Advanced Card Technologies Seminar (3)</li><li>Association of Canadian Travel Agents annual conference - technology panel</li><li>BC charity / loyalty program</li><li>BC retailers potential new loyalty program</li><li>Briefings on the North American marketplace for several corporations, including Post Bank and ING Bank of the Netherlands</li><li>Catherine Johnston and Joanne De Laurentiis were keynote speakers at the Credit Union Executives Conference - The Next Wave in Electronic Services: Where Will the Leaders Focus?</li><li>CIPs (VCR, Victoria) - Intro to technology seminars</li><li>Electronic Payment Systems and Smart Card Technology (Toronto) - chair + *Exploring the latest developments in smart card technology and their applications in business*</li><li>*e-money panel moderator* Canadian Payments Association stakeholder plenary meeting</li><li>IIR Conference speaker</li><li>*Potential uses for smart cards* Canadian Airlines</li><li>Privacy Seminar</li><li>Racing to the Future with Smart Cards</li><li>RBC Entertainment closed purse system</li><li>Retailers' Symposium</li><li>*The use of advanced cards in the travel industry and cards in the pockets of travelers keynote* Canadian Travel & Technology Conference</li></ul>

Key Additional Member Services	External Events (other)	Affiliations
<ul><li>Board institutes an annual awards program</li><li>Canadian Payments Association conference planning committee member</li><li>Established web based communication portals for: telephony special interest group (SIG), Mondex Unattended Point of Sale Task Force, smart cards on the internet SIG and the Global Stored Value Supplier Forum</li><li>Meeting of retailers, bankers and technologists together to discuss the evolving payment system in Canada</li><li>Members' only page launched</li><li>Work with a member consortium on ground breaking multi-application smart card system</li></ul>	<ul><li>Barrie Ontario to discuss Visa Cash with merchants and consumers</li><li>CardTech/SecurTech</li><li>Global Chip Card Alliance meeting (Long Beach)</li><li>Global Mondex Supplier meeting (Washington)</li></ul>	<ul><li>ACT Canada becomes a founding member of the newly formed Smart Card Global Summit – later known as ISCAN – the International Smart Card Associations Network</li></ul>

Government Appointments	Government Key Consultations	Government Key Interactions
<ul><li>Canadian Payments Association – Stakeholders Advisory Council</li><li>Gov of Ontario appoints ACT Canada to sit on the Secure Electronic Access Card Advisory Board Council (SEAC)</li><li>Industry Canada names ACT Canada as a conduit for information</li></ul>	<ul><li>ACT mounted a successful campaign to change the stored value definition as written by the CPA in a submission to the federal government.</li><li>BC Privacy Commissioner's staff - briefing on stored value</li><li>Corrections Canada consulted us about two proposed stored value card systems for Canada's newest penitentiary</li><li>Federal Privacy Commissioner's office asks ACT Canada to review and respond to the report entitled, "The Protection of Personal Information" from the task force on Electronic Commerce, a joint initiative of Industry Canada and the Department of Justice Canada</li><li>Justice and Industry Canada asks ACT Canada to consult on federal government privacy legislation (C6 - PIPEDA)</li><li>Ontario government asks ACT Canada to consult on privacy legislation</li></ul>	<ul><li>Closed door session with members of the Ontario government Management Board Secretariat and the Ministry of Health</li><li>Gov of Cda invites ACT Canada to participate in Canada / France roundtable trade discussions</li><li>OECD meeting - steering committee</li></ul>

1997 Key highlights...

- Through web based communication portals and other services, ACT Canada helped members focus on emerging market opportunities for:
  - telephony
  - special interest group (SIG),
  - Mondex Unattended Point of Sale Task Force,
  - smart cards on the internet SIG and
  - the Global Stored Value Supplier Forum

Metrics

- 25 member events and workgroups
- 11 publications/reports/papers
- 16 speeches
- 8 government consultations / appointments, key interactions

The market...

- Mondex in Guelph, Visa Cash in Barrie, Exact in Kingston and Bell Canada's Quick Change all bring heat to an emerging market
- There is international interest from European FIs in how Canada is progressing with smart cards
- Interest broadens as airlines and entertainment groups look at the potential of smart cards Quebec gets ready to roll out a smart health card
- Capacitive cards roll out in several BC cities for transit

Board of Directors

Joyce Bodner	ACT Canada
Joanne Boyar	RBA
Joanne De Laurentiis	Interac
Paul de Rosse	Verifone
John Ellis	Credit Union Central of Canada
Dawn Gallagher	BA Custom Cards
Dianne Gannon	Royal Bank
Alan Gavan	Security Card Systems
Wendy Hope	Canadian Payments Association
Catherine Johnston	ACT Canada
Greg McKenzie	Security Card Services Group
Pam Peck	Visa Canada
Ralph Sutton	Blackhall
Peter Uehlecke	SGS Thomson

ACT Canada notes of interest

- As the market emerges, ACT Canada takes on new roles, becoming a driving force
- World's first Privacy Impact Assessment Procedure for Advanced Card Applications (co-authored with the Information and Privacy Commission, Ontario)
- Publishes Financial Post supplement - Make way for advanced cards
- The association formally complains to CBC regarding their Channel Zero Mondex program, citing incomplete and biased information

1997

Bringing members together and building an informed market

ACT Canada Member Events, Teams and Workgroups	Publications, Reports, Papers & Media	Speeches, Briefings
<ul><li>An Introduction to Advanced Card Technologies Seminar (Hamilton)</li><li>Annual General Meeting</li><li>Canadian e-Cash pilots review</li><li>Cardware 1997: Killer Applications, Hot Technologies & Strategic Directions (Hamilton)</li><li>Global Stored Value Suppliers' Forum (work group) launched</li><li>Introduction to Advanced Card Technologies Seminar</li><li>Mondex Suppliers Forum (Guelph)</li><li>Patron's reception</li><li>Privacy and Technology Seminar</li><li>Smart Card Education workgroup (monthly lunch and learns)</li><li>Smart Card Information Exchange group</li><li>Smart Cards, Privacy and Emerging Card Technologies seminars (Toronto, Hamilton, Halifax)</li><li>Stored Value work group</li></ul>	<ul><li>*A Year of Growth for Canada* SCTI journal</li><li>ACTion bulletins</li><li>*Financial Post supplement - Make way for advanced cards*, 1st nationally distributed good news about advanced card technologies</li><li>Global TV and other media coverage of Privacy Impact Assessment launch</li><li>*Members Directory*</li><li>Montreal Gazette - Quebec ID cards, CJAD (Mtl) and CBC radio</li><li>Province (BC) - e-cash interview</li><li>*Smart, Optical and Other Advanced Cards: How to do a Privacy Assessment* co-authored with the Information and Privacy Commission, Ontario (world's first)</li><li>*What Is the Right to Privacy With Respect To Non-Internet Applications (Technology of Privacy or Technology of Surveillance?)*</li></ul>	<ul><li>*Advanced Card Technology: The turn of the century and beyond* Canadian Financial Services in the 21st Century</li><li>An Introduction to Advanced Card Technologies Seminar – instructor</li><li>Cardware 1997</li><li>CPA Conference Chart Your Course: Set Sail for 2000 and Beyond (Halifax) - co-chair</li><li>IIR Conference – ½ day seminar</li><li>Introduction to Advanced Card Technologies Seminar</li><li>*Is there a need for identity cards?* Privacy conference</li><li>Privacy and Technology Seminar</li><li>*Smart Cards and Tourism* Conference Board (Niagara on the Lake)</li><li>*Smart Cards, Privacy and Emerging Technologies* (3)</li><li>*Smart cards: efficiency vs confidentiality* 1st International Privacy conference</li><li>*Stored value* BAI (Bank Administration Institute) conference (Dallas)</li><li>*Trans border movement of persons, goods and information using advanced cards* Canadian Club of Chicago</li><li>*What is the right to privacy with respect to non-internet applications (technology of privacy or technology of surveillance?)* 1st Annual Human Rights and Information Technology Conference</li></ul>

Key Additional Member Services	External Events (other)

- CIBC Executive briefing
- Smart card education group launched

- Commercial Biometric Developer Consortium (founding meetings
- CT/ST
- Global Privacy Conference (Mtl)

Government Appointments	Government Key Consultations	Government Key Interactions

- Canadian Payments Association – Stakeholders Advisory Council
- Industry Canada names ACT Canada as the conduit for all requests from consulates or international organizations in relationship to advanced card technologies
- National Advisory Board on Tourism and Technology (federal government appointment)

- Commissioner's office (IPC/O)
- Status of Disabled Persons / Standing Committee of Human Rights roundtable discussions on privacy - Senator Joyce Fairburn chair

- Developed the world's first the Privacy Impact Assessment Procedure for smart card applications the Ontario Privacy with the Information and Privacy Commissioner (Ontario)
- Industry Canada asks ACT to speak at the France - Canada roundtable trade discussions (Vancouver) - The State of the Smart Card Industry in Canada
- NABTT work group to identify training required in travel and tourism to meet the needs of evolving advanced card technology applications

1996 Key highlights...

Through the association's International Advisory Board, Ottawa Special Interest Group, Electronic Commerce Applications committee, Information Exchange committee, as well as other services, ACT Canada helped members focus on emerging market opportunities and confront a major issue.

Metrics

- 13 member events and workgroups
- 8 publications/reports/papers
- 22 speeches / briefings
- 7 government consultations / appointments, key interactions

The market...

- A for-profit Canadian company trademarks the term "smart card" and the industry turns to ACT Canada to resolve the conflict
- Talks move from where smart cards are headed to where they are already in use and actual applications, not just technology
- Privacy issues arise in the market
- American Express, Interac, MasterCard and Visa Canada develop common specifications for Canadian integrated circuit cards using EMV documents and 7816

Board of Directors

Chris Asimakis	Security Card Systems
Steve Baker	Chrysalis ITS
Joyce Bodner	ACT Canada
John Courtney	BA Custom Cards
Floyd Diaz	AES Prodata
John Ellis	Credit Union Central of Canada
Dianne Gannon	Royal Bank
Brock Hansler	Brinks SFB Solutions Ltd
Brian Harding	Toronto Stock Exchange
Gerry Henderson	RBA Inc
Gerald Hubbard	Micro Card Technologies Inc
Steve Jones	Stentor Resource Centre
Catherine Johnston	ACT Canada
Scott Magnacca	NBS Card Services
Terry McLouglin	CDSL
Ralph Sutton	Blackhall Smartech Inc
Daniel Tardif	Oberthur Canada Inc

ACT Canada notes of interest

- membership expands to include companies from the US, Australia and Europe
- the association takes a proactive approach to privacy issues
- the first web site – www.actcda.com -is launched
- June 96, Board promotes C Johnston to President from COO
- membership exceeds 65
- conference delegates use stored value smart cards in vending machines
- ACT Canada issues world's first Halloween themed prepaid card to conference delegates

1996

Bringing members together and building an informed market

ACT Canada Member Events, Teams and Workgroups	Publications, Reports, Papers & Media	Speeches, Briefings
- An Introduction to Advanced Card Technology Seminars (Halifax and Toronto) - Annual Conference (Toronto) - Annual General Meeting - Electronic Commerce Applications committee - Information Exchange committee - International Advisory Board - Killer Applications & Hot Technologies Conference (Vancouver) - Ottawa Special Interest Group - Plan for the Future - An Exercise in Influence Seminar - Privacy Seminars (Halifax and Toronto) - Spring symposium	- ACTion Bulletin newsletter - *For BC it's all in the cards* BC Province - *Bellcore Labs report on smart cards debunked* - *Electronic Cash, Commerce and Mondex* EDI Forum - *Glossary of Terms* - *Biometrics and cashless payment* HUM (government computer magazine) - www.actcda.com, the association's first web site is launched - Various media about the proposed Quebec ID card	- ACT Canada Spring symposium - ACTA – Alliance of Canadian Travel Associations committee - An Introduction to Advanced Card Technology Seminars (Halifax and Toronto) - Annual Conference (Toronto) - Annual General Meeting - *Smart Cards – Trends and Developments* Conference Board of Canada - *Smart cards and stored value* CPA Stakeholders Advisory Council - *Plastic in the electronic world* EDI - e-commerce strategies - ICM Bank Fraud conference - conference chair and speaker - *The motivators and obstacles of smart card usage in Canada* IIR conference - *Intro to technology* IIR seminar - Information Systems Control Association - Mastercard/Visa standards - Killer Applications & Hot Technologies Conference (Vancouver) - Market briefings (Corporate Presentations program) to senior execs of Mutual of Omaha, Bowne + Prior Data (Spar Aerospace) - Plan for the Future - An Exercise in Influence Seminar - Privacy Seminars (Halifax and Toronto) - *Smart Cards for Airlines* presentation to reps of 85 airlines - *Keynote speech* Stentor Managers Planning Conference (Ottawa)

Key Additional Member Services	External Events (other)
▪ Corporate Presentations program is launched	▪ CT/ST (San Jose)

Government Appointments	Government Key Consultations	Government Key Interactions
▪ Canadian Payments Association, Stakeholders Advisory Council ▪ National Advisory Board on Tourism and Technology (federal government appointment)	▪ Parliamentary Committee for the Status of Disabled Persons	▪ BC Lottery Corporation ▪ Canadian Payments Association – Stakeholder plenary ▪ Canadian Space Agency ▪ Nova Scotia Economic Renewal Agency

1995 Key highlights...

- Post-recession, ACT Canada concentrates on building an informed market where members can achieve their goals.

Metrics

- 3 member events and workgroups
- 5 publications/reports/papers
- 5 speeches
- 3 government consultations / appointments, key interactions

The market...

- Mondex Canada is announced in May
- Talks move from where smart cards are headed to where they are already in use and actual applications, not just technology
- Privacy issues arise in the market
- Europay International S.A., Master Card International Incorporated and Visa International Service Association issue EMV specs - Integrated Circuit Card Specifications for Payment Systems (3 parts)
- Members of Visa, MasterCard and Interac form the Canadian Chip Card Committee to develop the IMV specs - common standards and specifications which would support the introduction of chip cards in Canada
- Fraud is a growth industry, Canada currently is 3 times world average, deemed to be "safe" for crooks
- Smart card prices dropping approximately 10% per year
- Telecommunications, banking, transportation and government are all sectors actively looking at smart cards

Board of Directors

Joyce Bodner	*ACT Canada*
John Ellis	*Credit Union Central of Canada*
Catherine Johnston	*ACT Canada*
Steve Jones	*Stentor Resource Centre*
Kelly Kilga	*CTST*
Scott Magnacca	*NBS Card Services*
Terry McLouglin	*CDSL*

ACT Canada notes of interest

- ACT represents the Canadian marketplace at conferences from Paris to Hong Kong
- the association becomes active in travel and tourism sector
- the association's mandate expands
- conference grows 200% from '94

1995

Bringing members together and building an informed market

ACT Canada Member Events, Teams and Workgroups	Publications, Reports, Papers & Media	Speeches
▪ Annual General Meeting ▪ Awards ▪ Building the Business Case for Advanced Technologies Conference	▪ ACTion Bulletin newsletters ▪ *Hitting the ground running: Canada joins the smart card world* Smart Card Technology International journal ▪ *Market Facts study* ▪ Midday (CBC) ▪ *Privacy, Smart Cards and Healthcare* SCTRA	▪ *Advanced Card Technologies: is there a business case for Canada?* Canadian Payments Association ▪ *Smart Cards for health care and their impact on streamlining the system* Healthcare's Powershift: Using Technology for excellence and efficiency ▪ *Smart Cards: the battle between banks and technology companies for global market share in electronic-cash products* New Delivery Channels for Financial Services ▪ *Technology and Tourism Possibilities* Alliance of Travel Associations (Hong Kong) ▪ *The State of the Canadian Marketplace* Cartes

Key Additional Member Services	External Events (other)
▪ Awards	▪ Biometrics Industry Standards Association (Washington) ▪ CTST ▪ Cartes

Government Appointments	Government Key Consultations	Government Key Interactions
▪ National Advisory Board on Tourism and Technology (federal government appointment)	▪ Alberta Privacy Commission	▪ Ontario Hospital Association

NOTE: most of the records for 1995 could not be found. The information above was culled from variety of sources and does not represent all the work done in this year.

1994 Key highlights...

- Bylaws require members to vote to keep the association open, due to the original "sunset" clause
- George Brown College asks permission to distribute ACT's smart cards and healthcare paper to health care students and include questions from the paper on students' exams
- The mandate is expanded to include complimentary technologies such as biometrics
- Membership grows 350% from '93
- Membership is by invitation only
- ACT launches speakers program, in-house and external publishing, seminars and annual conference
- Another association applies to the Ontario provincial government for funding to take over the work of ACT Canada, without any discussion with us. Funding was not forthcoming and we moved on.

Metrics

- 5 member events, teams and workgroups
- 2 publications/reports/papers
- 10 speeches
- 3 government appointments / consultations / key interactions

The market...

- Market interest in advanced card technologies grows
- Healthcare leads the pack related to potential applications
- Privacy and security related to advanced card technologies both become topics of interest to governments as they look at applications ranging from automatic toll collection, inventory control, health cards, benefit payments, passports and LAN security devices
- UBI interactive cable project announces smart card based payment and access via TV sets
- A large transit authority announces the use of smart cards for revenue sharing and assessment – a first in transit
- Smart cards become more powerful and less expensive
- Bell Canada, Mississauga Transit, Quebec Health Card and the Toronto Zoo all have smart card plans
- MasterCard states their intention to move to a smart card based platform
- Interac completes an extensive review of enhanced card technologies
- The overall level of credit card fraud for Canadian Visa and MasterCard issuers has nearly tripled, from $28.9 million in 1990 to over $75 million in 1993. Counterfeit fraud represents over 30% of fraud for some issuers.

Board of Directors

Arnaud d'Avezac	Micro Card Technologies
Rene Bastien	Nova Services Conseils
Joyce Bodner	Deisel Farms
Floyd Diaz	Datafare
John Ellis	Credit Union Central of Canada
Catherine Johnston	Johnston/Belanger
Terry McLoughlin	CDSL
Robert Silc	Power Vision Data Systems
Steve Zolnierczyk	Management Board Secretariat (Ont)

1994

Bringing members together and building an informed market

ACT Canada Member Events, Teams and Workgroups	Publications, Reports, Papers & Media	Speeches
• Advanced Cards 101 Halifax, Ottawa and Calgary • Annual General Meeting • Cards/Cards/Cards Conference (Toronto) • Seminars (Halifax, Calgary, Ottawa)	• ACTION Canada newsletter • *Smart Cards and Healthcare*	• *Advanced Cards 101* Halifax, Ottawa and Calgary • Cards/Cards/Cards Conference (Toronto) • EDI Conference • Insite Conference on Healthcare • Privacy and Technology - The role of government in the electronic world – panelist (Ottawa) • Privacy Issues (Ottawa) • *Smart Cards* ITAC Information Strategies and Emerging Technologies for Healthcare • Technology and Tourism workshop

Key Additional Member Services	External Events (other)	Government Key Appointment
• Free passes for the Palm/Laptop Expo	• CardTech / SecurTech • EDI conference - booth	• Federal Government appoints ACT Canada to the National Advisory Board on Tourism and Technology

Government Key Consultations
• Federal Privacy Commissioner's office asks ACT to review their "Privacy and Smart Cards Framework" • RCMP ask ACT to review their Threat Risk Analysis of Smart Cards

1989 - 1993 Key highlights...

The market gets off to a strong start and then stalls.

1989

- ACT Canada is incorporated February 16, 1989
    - It is formed to provide "a forum for the exchange of ideas and information on card technology for the mutual benefit of suppliers and users of all types of cards, supporting equipment and software related to the development and application of electronic methods of carrying out business"
- An Executive Director is hired to build the association
- 1st AGM and 1st elected board
- Focus on healthcare, transportation, social assistance payments and the role of smart and optical cards

1990

- Market trials range from physical access to access to services.
- Active sectors include banking, health care, transportation, communications and others

1991

- A serious restructuring in the smart card industry, particularly in the US, raises questions about the continued viability of the technology
- Catherine Johnston is elected Chairman of the Board
- Advanced card technologies are of more interest to technical than business people
- Both Quebec and Ontario conduct smart card trials
- The federal government has a Smart Card Task Force

1992

- The association enjoys strong initial growth hitting a high of 62 members in 1992. Then a recession hits and membership falls to 18.
- ACT continues to provide information and education to build awareness
- Healthcare remains a focus for the association
- ACT Canada serves as a pipeline for information and contacts
- The association also focusses on advocacy and awareness

1993

- The market recession hits the association hard. Assets, consisting of a large metal filing cabinet, files and the association's phone number, are moved into Catherine Johnston's basement. The rebuilding of the association starts after a brief period of self-imposed "hibernation".
- Government and Transportation are the leading sectors for smart card applications
- Companies and governments start to look for fresh ideas as the recession starts to wind down
- Metrics
  - 5 member events, teams and workgroups
  - 2 publications/reports/papers
  - 10 speeches
  - 3 government appointments / consultations / key interactions

Founding Board of Directors (1989 – 1990)

David Antebi	IBM Canada Limited
Lorne Boates	DB Systems Information Exchange Inc.
Martyn Cooper	Royal Bank of Canada
Paul Fisher	Royal Bank of Canada
Sonja Halvorson	Bull HN Information Systems Ltd.
Dr. Eric Meddings	Information Systems – Human Engineering
Stephen Price-Francis	The Optical Recording Company
Brendan Seaton	Carelink Inc.
Emerson Thorne	National Business Systems Inc

Legal Counsel
Martin Campbell   *Beard, Winter, Barristers and Solicitors*

1990 - 1991 Board

Rene Bastien	Raymond, Chabot, Martin, Pare
Sherry Connolly	Royal Trust
Martyn Cooper	Royal Bank
Geoff Crellin	CIBC
Dr Eric Meddings	Information Systems – Human Engineering
Ron Nicholson	Bell MediaTel
Stephen Price-Francis	The Optical Card Works
Brendan Seaton	Carelink
Emerson Thorne	E Thorne

1991 – 1992 board

Rene Bastien	Raymond, Chabot, Martin, Pare
Joyce Bodner	Ministry of Community and Social Services (Ont)
Catherine Johnston	Bull HN Information Systems
David Martin	Health and Welfare Canada
Stephen Price-Francis	Canon Canada Inc
Roy Rennicks	JNL International
Brendan Seaton	Carelink
Paul Smith	Bank of Montreal
Ron Sypher	TD Bank

1992 - 1993 Board

Joyce Bodner	Diesel Farms
John Ellis	Credit Union Central of Canada
Catherine Johnston	Johnston/Belanger
Jose Kapon	Powervision
Terry McLoughlin	CDSL
Mike Ozerkevitch	Strasys
Brian Pelley	Management Consultant
Kathleen Rivera	Rivera Hartling
Robert Silc	Powervision
Steve Zolnierczuk	Management Board Secretariat (Ont)

ACT Canada Member Events, Teams and Workgroups	Publications, Reports, Papers & Media	Speeches
1993 • Advanced Card Technologies for the '90s (Toronto, Ottawa) • Annual Conference (Toronto) • Annual General Meeting • Ottawa Special Interest group	• ACTION Canada newsletter (4) • *Privacy for EFT*	• *Advanced Card Technologies for the '90s (updated)* • Annual Conference • CardTech/SecurTech
1992 • ACT is represented on the ISO Canadian Advisory Committee and several workgroups • Annual General Meeting • Canadian Smart Cards Standards Steering Committee member • Health Special Interest Group • Ottawa Special Interest Group	• *1992 Directory of Members' Goods and Services* • ACT issues the *Canadian Advanced Card Technology Market Study* • ACTION Canada newsletter (4) • *Advanced Card Applications for Retail and Transportation* • *Contactless Smart Cards and other advanced card technologies* • *Cost justification for advanced card technologies* • *Smart Card Applications and Pilots* • *Smart Card Security and Physical Characteristics* • *What is a memory card?*	• *Advanced Card Technologies for the '90s* • EDI Conference
1991 • 1st Annual General Meeting • Canadian Smart Card Standards SIG (responsibility and funding assumed by CPA) • Symposium '91 Annual Conference (Toronto) – keynote speaker Roland Moreno	• *1991 Directory of Members' Goods and Services* • ACTION Canada newsletter (4)	• Symposium '91 Annual Conference
1990 • Annual General Meeting • 2nd Annual Symposium • Canadian Smart Cards Standards Special Interest Group launched	• *1990 Directory of Services* • ACTION Canada newsletter (4)	• Cardtech
1989 • Advanced Card Applications Symposium '89 • Canadian Smart Cards Standards SIG • First founding members meeting	• Newsletter launched (4)	• Advanced Card Applications Symposium '89 • SCAT conference

Key Additional Member Services	External Events (other)

1993
- ACT is represented on ISO Canadian Advisory Committee

- CardTech / SecurTech – drop in session

1992
- ACT Canada study results in move to establish financial transaction standards to complement international standards (the Canadian Smart Card Standards)

- CardTech / SecurTech
- EDI Conference – partner event
- IIR conference
- Plastic Card Conference (PACE)

1991
- ACT is represented on ISO Canadian Advisory Committee

- Canadian Payments Association Conference
- CardTech
- Consumers" Association of Canada's Cards, Cards, Cards
- SCAT
- World Conference on Patient Cards

Government Key Consultations	Government Key Interactions

1993
- Province of Ontario starts to talk with ACT Canada about smart cards

- ACT Canada distributes the City of Calgary RFI for parking permits to members
- External Affairs meeting (Information Technology and Environmental Industry division)

1992
- Attorney General's office discussions re changing legislation governing use of electronic data in presenting evidence

1991
- Ministry of Health (Ont) briefing on health member and card legislation (2nd)
- Ontario Health Insurance ACT, Submission on Bill 24

- Canada Evidence Act – discussions about modification of the Act to enable the use of smart cards

1990
- Ontario Ministry of Health briefing on health member and card legislation

Appendix B – Acronyms, Alliances & Web Sites

Acronyms

AI	artificial intelligence
APEC	French Association of Card Manufacturers
BAC	ACT Canada Board Advisory Committee
BoBs	ACT Canada Business Opportunity Bulletins
CAC	ISO Canadian Advisory Committee
CAMA	Canadian Automatic Merchandising Association
CAN-ID	Report on Visons for Canadian Identity Policy
CATSA	Canadian Air Transport Security Authority
CCECE	Canadian Conference on Electrical and Computer Engineering
CFLA	Canadian Finance and Leasing Association
CIPs	Canada's Association of IT Professionals
CNP	card not present
CPA	Canadian Payments Association - now Payments Canada
CRA	Canada Revenue Agency
CTST	CardTech/SecurTech (conferences)
CTST Canada	ACT Canada conference branding for 2 years
CUCC	Credit Union Central of Canada
CUTA	Canadian Urban Transit Association
CWTA	Canadian Wireless Telecommunications Association
DCC	dynamic currency conversion
DND	Canadian Department of National Defense
DOD	US Department of Defense
eCommerce	electronic commerce
EDI	electronic data interchange
EESTEL	Association of European Experts in E-Transactions Systems
EFT	electronic funds transfer
EMV	EuroPay MasterCard Visa
EMVCo	facilitator of worldwide interoperability and acceptance of secure payment transactions
e-payments	electronic payments
ESD	electro-static discharge
ETA	Electronic Transactions Association
FCAC	Financial Consumer Agency of Canada
FinPay	Finance Canada Payments Consultative Committee
Fintrac	Financial Transactions and Reports Analysis Centre of Canada
GCCA	Global Chip Card Alliance
GSMA	Global System for Mobile Communications
GTEC	Government and Technology conference
HCE	host card emulation
HRDC	Human Resources Development Canada
IBIA	International Biometrics Industry Association

ICC	Institute for Canadian Citizenship / integrated circuit chip
ICMA	International Card Manufacturers Association
IEEE	Institute of Electrical and Electronics Engineers
IIR	Institute for International Research
IMS-MTE	Integrated Mobility Systems - Moving the Economy
IoT	internet of things
IPC/O	Information and Privacy Commissioner / Ontario
iPOS	internet point of sale
IPSI	Identity, Privacy and Security Institute at the University of Toronto
IRUG	IBM retail users group
ISAAC	ICT Standards Advisory Council of Canada
ISCAN	International Smart Card Associations Network
ISO	International Standards Organization
ITAC	International Technology Association of Canada
LL&A	Luggage, Leathergoods and Accessories Magazine
MAG	Merchant Advisory Group
MAOSCO	the Secretariat body of the MULTOS Consortium
mCommerce	mobile conference
MoSLT	ACT Canada Mobile Strategic Leadership team
mPOS	mobile point of sale
MRC	Merchant Risk Council
NABTT	National Advisory Board for Technology and Tourism
NACCU	National Association of Campus Card Users
NFC	near field communications
NIIC	ACT Canada's National Issuers and Infrastructure Committee
OBSI	Ombudsman for Banking Services and Investments
OECD	Organisation for Economic Co-operation and Development
P2P	person to person payment
P2PE	point to point encryption
PAC	ACT Canada President's Advisory Council
PIA	Privacy Impact Assessment
PIPEDA	Personal Information Protection and Electronic Documents Act
PKI	public key infrastructure
POS	point of sale
RCMP	Royal Canadian Mounted Police
RFID	radio frequency identification
SAC	Stakeholder Advisory Council - CPA
SCA	Smart Card Alliance
SCTI	Smart Card Technology International (journal)
SEAC	Gov't of Ontario Secure Electronic Access Card Advisory Board
TEE	trusted execution environment
TMAC	Treasury Management Association of Canada
WIP	ACT Canada's Women in Payment

Alliances

AFPC	Association des Fabricants et Personnalisateurs de Cartes
ATMIA	ATM Industry Association
CAMA	Canadian Automatic Merchandising Association
Cartes	
CAC	Consumers Association of Canada
CPPO	Canadian Prepaid Providers Organization
CUTA	Canadian Urban Transit Association
EMVCo	
EESTEL	Association of European Experts in E-Transactions Systems
ETA	Electronic Transactions Association
Eurosmart	
Global Platform	
ICMA	International Card Manufacturers Association
IMS-MTE	Integrated Mobility Systems - Moving the Economy
ITAC	International Technology Association of Canada
Law Enforcement (federal, provincial, local)	
MAG	Merchant Advisory Group
MCX	Merchant Customer Exchange
NACCU	National Association of College Card Users
Payments Business Magazine	
Payments Canada (formerly Canadian Payments Association)	
PMAC	Purchasing Management Association of Canada (PMAC)
Retail Merchant Associations	
SCAFI – Smart Card Forum of India	
Smart Card Alliance	
Smart Card Forum of China	
Smart Card Society of Southern Africa	

Web sites

www.actcda.com
emvcanada.ca/com
emv-usa.ca/com
secure-gov-id.com

Appendix C - ACT Canada

This book is not about ACT Canada, but there is no denying that the association has a long history of bringing stakeholders together to shape the payment and digital ID markets. Should you be a member? Probably, but take a few minutes to read this appendix and then you'll have enough information to decide.

Do you want to...?

- Have access to others who can impact you and who share many of your goals and obstacles to:
  - ✓ share information in the context of your market – a good way to leverage your research resources
  - ✓ ensure that they understand your needs, goals and processes – so that they don't inadvertently take steps that will negatively impact you
  - ✓ help you succeed with your plans and projects
- Set direction on priority issues
- Influence key market initiatives
- Work with others on non-competitive issues
- Work with other stakeholders to understand their processes and/or concerns and propose solutions
- Publish widely read thought-leadership papers
- Gain In-depth and timely exposure to the industry's best practices
- Hear multiple stakeholder perspectives
- Achieve personal and professional satisfaction from making a difference and
- Network with market shapers

ACT Canada enables all of these.

What's the benefit?

- Talking with others who have a stake in payment has many benefits:
  - ✓ Ideas are shared and differing perspectives are offered when you are with a group. The words, "I hadn't thought of that" or "Now that you say that, it makes me think..." are indicators of value.
  - ✓ Insights can come from a conversation with a colleague or in a meeting. The more people gathered together to discuss a common interest, the greater the likelihood that you will gain insight. And when you open your world to new people who share your interests, you stand an even better chance of learning from them.
  - ✓ Creative, collaborative thought - the type that happens when someone hears something and responds verbally. You just can't do that in email.

How benefits are delivered

- Strategic Leadership teams
- Networking Events – both informal and structured
- Subject Matter Expert Speakers – providing timely information and looking at subjects from a fresh viewpoint
- Insights gleaned from 28 years of experience and a global network
- ... and many other services

Strategic Leadership Teams

Digital wallets, mobile payment, apps, prepaid and gift cards, blockchain, biometric authentication, digital currency, IoT payments and artificial intelligence (AI) are all opportunities for the majority of ACT Canada members.

Most of the research each does is substantially the same as the others so ACT Canada brings members together to advance their knowledge through strategic leadership teams. This approach saves members both time and money.

Not only do team members learn from each other and the research done by subgroups, they often publish papers that provide focused and timely information to other members.

Essentially, SLTs help members:

- simplify complex issues
- facilitate resolutions to market / industry wide problems
- separate truth from all the market noise and hype
- get the big picture
- understand the nuances and
- make informed decisions

Today they are called Strategic Leadership teams but they have been known by other terms over the years. Here are the *member-driven teams* from the past and the papers they have published. It will give you some insight into what the market has looked at since 1995.

- *Customer Authentication*: Strong Authentication & Payments: Stakeholder Perspectives, Report on What Determines an Authentication?/Identifying the Issues/Technology & Processes/Identifying the Players & Stakeholders/Requirements – Definitions, Customer Authentication SLT: Tokenization White Paper
- *Cyber Security for Payments*
- *Emerging Markets and Technologies*
- *Emerging Technologies, Applications and Markets:* Glossary of Terms
- *Emerging Technologies, Standards and Market*
- *EMV for the US:* USA EMV best practices for retailers
- *EMV Workgroup* (Canada): Best EMV Practices, EMV Whitepaper
- *Financial & Merchant*
- *Financial Services:* Public Awareness of Card Fraud Issues
- *Government Stakeholder Forum*
- *Government*: An Assessment of Business Liability & Risk associated with the implementation of the Community of Interest (CoI) concept, Privacy impact assessment of the collection and distribution of multi-program data through a community-of-interest service delivery system
- *ID*
- *Identity Management:* White Paper on Border Security
- *Infrastructure Forum*
- *Issues Alert team*
- *Issues Management Team (aka POS):* ESD Report
- *M-Commerce* (Mobile)
- *Merchant: Best EMV practices for merchants; Merchant Engagement report, Retailer Position Paper, Preparing Merchants for the Future of Payments*
- *Mobile:* Mobile report 2011, Mobile Blueprint, 10 documents, including a list

of market inhibitors, a watch list of potential regulatory influences and other pertinent information.

- *Multi-app Issuance*
- *National Card Advancement Committee*
- *National Issuers & Infrastructure Committee:* A New Partnership Approach to Business Applications, Infrastructure and Application Development Whitepaper, Business Rationale for PKI / Smart Card rollout Whitepaper, Consumer and Corporate Users Whitepaper, Design Considerations - A Business Perspective, Infrastructure Whitepaper, Privacy Whitepaper, Security Whitepaper
- *National Merchants Forum (workgroup)*

- *Payment Acceptance   (formerly POS)*
- *PIN Management:* RFP
- *Point of Sale:* Contactless Certification Stakeholder Impact Report
- *Prepaid and Gift cards*
- *Prepaid Cards*: Prepaid Report 2011
- *Privacy Protection*
- *Retail Forum*
- *Retail workgroup*
- *Retailer Stakeholder Forum Group*
- *Secure Chip   (with ITAC)*
- *Secure ID / Customer Authentication*; Secure ID Report 2011
- *Stakeholder*

Connecting people, enabling dialogue and driving insights - all continue to be highly valued by payment professionals, not just by those in Canada but by ACT Canada's entire global network.

Putting more weapons in your arsenal...

Knowledge transfer – this is a case where the sum of the parts is greater than the whole. The association helps:

- advance people's career's by giving them access to insights and market information, as well as training
- employers develop more knowledgeable staff
- payment stakeholders find solutions to barriers and issues
- employers show their commitment to staff through an investment in their training/education
- payment stakeholders successfully reach their goals

Insights - a deep understanding of persons or things. In the age of the internet the enemy is not too little information, but too much. According to the Economist the amount of data stored doubles every 18 months and data fatigue is cited as a source of stress, negatively impacting workers at all levels. Insights help you increase revenues, lower costs and reduce risk.

A google search of biometric authentication yields more than 1,320,000 hits in less than 1 second and yet very few if any of these sites can tell you the impact of bio-auth on issuers, acquirers, merchants, consumers and payment networks - but the association can because it understands the stakeholders, the market and the technology. It also has the ability to bring interested parties together to drive even more insights.

> "The fog of information can drive out knowledge." Daniel J Boorstin
> "A moment's insight is sometimes worth a life's experience." Oliver Wendell Holmes, Sr.

Advocacy – every year the association does a significant amount. Much of it is delivered through speeches and articles, government consultations and advisory boards.   Along with knowledge transfer, advocacy helps build an informed marketplace. Because payment continues to evolve there is a constant need for a trusted, neutral voice like ACT Canada's.

> *ACT Canada proactively educates members and acts as a trusted resource for public and private interests.*

Discounts – every year the association negotiates discounts for members to obtain research or to attend key conferences, as well as providing discounts for ACT Canada events, training, research and other services / products.

The bottom line...

Sometimes life may be like a box of chocolates, but more often it is like a thousand piece jigsaw puzzle. Each day we all work on pieces of various plans and projects. Can you imagine how difficult it would be to assemble that puzzle or manage that project if you didn't have a picture of the desired end result? Add to that the possibility that you might not have all the pieces. Some may be in the hands of other stakeholders.

Unless you believe you know everything, you can easily see the advantage of having other people give you useful information. It can be most valuable when it is a part of a dynamic conversation between two or more people and less valuable when it is static. Brainstorming sessions are designed to take advantage of dynamic thoughts that come from human interaction.

ACT Canada members have always valued opportunities to come together to:

- discuss ways to successfully meet their goals
- learn how to overcome obstacles
- understand complex issues
- develop relationships that can lead to future accomplishments

... and ACT Canada brings them together.

There are a lot of association,s but most of them focus on a single group or profession. ACT Canada works with many of them from around the world. They all have value, but bringing together payment stakeholder groups provides an unparalleled value.

We're all too busy

In 2011, SAS Canada & Leger marketing reported that 47% of Canadian executives say they are overwhelmed by information. Note - not overloaded, but "overwhelmed". Wikipedia defines overwhelmed as: 1. Buried or drowned beneath a huge mass. 2. Defeated completely.

More recently in a survey of 1409 chief executives around the world (PWC Global CEO survey 2016), those in the financial sector named the speed of technological change as one of the top three extremely concerning issues facing the industry.

Where one organization says it is so busy that it relies on ACT Canada's benefits, another says they are too busy to be members. Which is right?

We're all busy, but we can't afford to waste opportunities to expand our circle of knowledge, to seek out experts, talk with people you normally don't meet with and discuss new ideas. You'll be surprised at how refreshed you can feel and how much you can learn in a single day. This is one reason why it's good to be an association member, particularly when you are busy.

ACT Canada members will offer their knowledge, perspective and context. They will help you develop and refine your thoughts. If what you want to do includes or affects them, they are essential to your success.

"Careers – what's in this for you?"

Careers are like houses, built one brick at a time. Usually many tradesmen work on it, each adding their skill and knowledge and all contributing to the final vision of the architect.

In our careers the skilled tradesmen are the people we deal with, whether they are peers, superiors or subordinates. They work in our companies and in others. Sometimes they provide information we need. Other times it is insight, enthusiasm or inspiration.

They challenge our assumptions or ideas. Sometimes they seem to slam doors in our faces, forcing us to look for new ways to move ahead. This accounts for some of the hardest but best lessons.

All these people help build our careers and contribute to the success of our projects and companies.

Bringing people together to help members achieve their goals is one of ACT Canada's primary purposes. Join ACT, join the dialogue, help your career and help your organization.

Be an Insider and benefit from…

- privileged access to information
- networking with new and existing members of the community
- our insights - based on our knowledge and global network to help increase revenues, lower costs and reduce risk
- one-on-one discussions with members
- consulting help
- customized e-introductions
- knowing what clients and prospects are hearing and asking of experts and other suppliers
- opportunities to showcase your work to potential buyers, partners, investors and the people who influence the market
- discounts for research studies, training and international conferences
- focussed, as well as informal, networking events
- the right to initiate an SLT to meet your corporate needs
- visibility through speaking or exhibiting at the act forum (formerly Cardware) or at external conferences as arranged by the association
- ACTion News: Driving Insights - sharing members' accomplishments with a global audience

Moving forward

There will always be a need for a stakeholder association. In spite of the complexities in payments, when stakeholders have a way to talk together they get much closer to realizing their own goals.

If you have questions that start with:

How do I, Why would I, What do you think of, Who should I, When should I, Could you help us with, What is happening in / at / with, Where would I or What if - and they are chip related applications, technologies or markets, call ACT Canada.

A FINAL REMINDER

Don't underestimate the power of connecting with people and organizations that can favourably impact your success.

Don't undervalue the influence you have when you're able to talk with other stakeholders.

These connections and conversations will lead to insights that can get you to market quicker, drive more revenue and profit, and mitigate risks.

Working together – works!

About the author

A sought after speaker and prolific writer, Catherine Johnston has delivered more than 300 speeches and written more than 250 articles on the subject of payments and identity management.

Her career has focused on emerging technologies and the benefits they bring to Canadians and others. For 26 years she served as the head of ACT Canada, the stakeholder association whose members have a stake in secure payment and digital identity management. During that time she closely observed both the politics and practicalities of payment. She has worked with payment stakeholders; acquirers, issuers, merchants, payment networks and governments, regulators, suppliers and privacy advocates.

Currently she serves on the Advisory board of Quantum-Safe Canada and heads Chieftain Consulting.

Catherine is presently writing her next book introducing questions that must be asked and answered to improve your life. your career and your company's success.